From Sorcerer's Daughter to Daughter of the King

By Ivet Fortun

© Copyright 2023 Ivet Fortun
Edited by Cathy Rivers

ACKNOWLEDGMENTS

I thank my Lord for saving me from a life leading me directly to destruction. My heart is filled with joy as I see the rocky path the Lord has helped me travel. Thank you, Lord, for saving my life and that of my family. Thank you for loving me and for having rescued me from the darkness in which I lived.

I am grateful to my mother for teaching me to love unconditionally, work hard and never give up. I love you.

Thanks to my daughters for always being by my side. Together, we have experienced many difficult circumstances, and today we are here serving the Lord. I love them with all my heart.

Many thanks to my husband, Isaías Rodríguez, for helping me through the process of writing this book. Thank you for your patience, love, and wisdom. Thank you for your prayers and daily support.

I am grateful to my high school teacher at New Futures School, who told me: "One day, you will write a book." Thank you for believing in me and encouraging me during my first years in the United States.

Finally, many thanks to everyone who has kept me in their prayers, both those I know and those I don't. Your spiritual support is vital to me.

DEDICATION

This book is dedicated to my relatives in Cuba. I hope that through these pages, they will come to know the God who saved me from the darkness and showed me the light.

I dedicate this book to my mother for her unconditional love and for teaching me endurance and hard work.

I also dedicate this work to my three grandchildren, Eli, Jacob and Zoey. You will be the next generation of Jesus' disciples.

It is also dedicated to those people who are still living among the lies of the new age, the occult, and witchcraft. I hope they will open their minds and hearts to the truth of God's Word so they can be free from the darkness.

I pray that their eyes will be opened and they will embrace the truths of God's Word. I pray that they will turn away from the lies and deception of Satan, who wants nothing more than to keep them in bondage.

INTRODUCTION

If you are unfamiliar with God's word, I recommend reading this book along with a Bible where necessary so that some unclear concepts can be demystified. This way, you will be able to better understand the process of what God has done with me and with many others who have a testimony of salvation. Some concepts may be difficult to understand if you are not familiar with the gospel, but if you seek God with all your heart, He will guide you into all truth.

As you read this book I pray that the Lord will open your eyes and minister freedom into your life. If you have ever been involved in the occult or witchcraft world at the end of the day there are prayers to break any generational curses you may be dealing with.

If you are going through a difficult time and you still have not given your life to Jesus. At the end of the book there is also a salvation prayer. Making this prayer will break all work of darkness in your life and you will become part of the people of God.

1
IN THE HIGH SEA

THE DAY WE DECIDED to jump into the sea, everything seemed to have gone well. The raft was ready; my mother, stepfather, and 13-year-old brother were there, along with four other strangers who would suffer the same fate as us. The raft was nothing more than a piece of board, a kind of floating door. It consisted of six-by-four boards held together with nails and rope, and underneath, it had rubber tires that made it float.

I was skinny and usually shy, with an air of fragility when walking. My big eyes would fill almost my entire face if it weren't for the big mouth that made the competition. I looked a lot like my mother; from what everyone said, my mom was darker and with a wider nose. They called my mother La China because of her slightly slanted eyes, which testified to a past in which the Chinese arrived in Cuba and integrated into society to the point of rubbing shoulders with blacks.

I would always get jealous walking down the street next to my mom and seeing how countless men complimented her. It was understandable; my mom, despite her short stature, was very attractive. Her black skin and wasp waist did not go unnoticed.

That night my mom was extremely nervous; she had told her brother Joseito the date and time the raft would leave. He felt he wasn't going to make it on time, but he ended up not coming because he had a fateful appointment to fulfill his destiny. Years later he would be accused of throwing his wife from a building which landed him in prison for twenty years.

At about 9 PM, the group was preparing to launch the raft into the sea. With secrecy, we tried to do everything since we left the country clandestinely; when the piece of wood was in the water, the men began to row. It was a calm but dark night. You could breathe the aroma of the sea when it is calm. Everyone was calm, especially my brother, who was stuck in the hollow space between the wood and the tires. It was a space about twenty inches wide. They had put him lying there so the Cuban coast guards would not see him. In those days, the president of Cuba, Fidel Castro, had said on television that he would let out those who wanted to leave, but they could not take children. I was only fourteen, so my mom tried to pass me off as an adult by letting my hair down and putting on some makeup.

The first hours passed in silence. But from one moment to the next, the sea began to move as if it were a runaway horse. The waves rose and fell, moving the raft in an excruciating way. And the darkness was possibly the scariest thing about it all. A few drops of rain began to fall. My mother hugged me, and I thought for a fleeting moment that everything would end. Nobody said anything, but the silence said it all. I began to pray with such intensity as I had never done before. I swore to God that I would give my life to serve him without giving details of that promise. Maybe I thought I would become a nun, donate exorbitant amounts of money, or maybe do sporadic volunteer work. At the time, I didn't think about it. There was no time to think about it. I just prayed continuously until I didn't know how long it was until the sea had given up its fury. I figured it was yemaya's work. My mother constantly repeated that she was the daughter of this deity, and perhaps that is why she was terrified of the sea. Yemaya is an Afro-Cuban folklore idol that is characterized by a woman dressed in blue. Her believers say that she rules the waters and everything in them.

I remember that sometimes, my mother never bathed in the sea when we went to the beach. She only dared to put the tips of her feet in, sometimes up to the ankles. A sudden memory came to my mind: I saw my mother "la china" with pink pants that she had rolled up to her knees to put her feet in the water of that beach. Suddenly some friends lifted her and threw her into the water. Mom came out of the water, pretending to be angry. The memory of that joke brought a smile back to my face. The night passed quietly after that scare. A few words were exchanged, and the darkness prevented communication using our glances.

With the first brushstrokes of dawn, everyone's spirits seemed to revive. Perhaps it was the immense gratitude for having survived such an uncertain night. In the group was a man with light brown hair, not exactly blond. He was a Jehovah's Witness and soon began to talk about religion. My ears were listening to the conversation, which was becoming livelier each time, but I was thinking of other things. I had heard of many people who had drowned trying the same trajectory. And of many other people who had seen bodies floating and even sharks that ate people. Surprisingly she was more excited than scared. I looked at the hole where my brother laid. A small boy, despite him being twelve years, with skin much whiter than everyone on the raft and medium curly hair and eyes like my mother, a little slanted, they called my brother mulatto blanco nazo because his skin was too white to be considered mulatto, and his hair was too curly to be considered white. Sometimes, they also considered me a mulatto if I had my hair combed and groomed. But if someone didn't like me or wanted to offend my mom, they considered me Jaba. I never understood the sin of being a Jaba; I heard people say they were light-skinned people with kinky hair. I remembered that my mother had at least one sister nicknamed Jaba. Her name was Olga but people called her Olguita. She was robust and worked in construction, hoping the government would give her one of the apartments in the many buildings she had helped build. After a few years, she managed to get one. She had two children, Belqui and Maiquel, a girl and a boy, respectively.

When it was already daylight, they took my brother out of the uncomfortable hole where he was hiding. His hands were wrinkled like an old man's from the humidity. The danger had passed, and he could now come out of hiding. We concluded that we were far enough from the island. Away from my dad, whom I loved so much, away from my friends, the rest of my family, everything I knew, and above all, away from Zacarias. He had been the boy closest to me in Cuba. I had that moment so present. I swore to myself that I would never forget that moment as long as I lived.

My mother had traded our house in Mantilla for a small room the size of a European bathroom in Old Havana, in a building that dates back to the colonial era. In that building, there was a large roof terrace where the tenants hung their clothes and sometimes stood on the balcony to watch passersby. From time to time, someone shouted: The fish has arrived! On that roof one night, my mother caught me kissing Zacarías with a passion that was inappropriate for my young age, as my mother considered. The boy was two years younger than me and just as shy and inexperienced. That night my mom slapped me, and I cried with rage because I was sure my stepfather had ratted me out. That wasn't enough for me, as a few days later, I found myself lying on the terrace once again on a few sheets under the starry sky, and hugging my back from behind was that mulatto boy with hazel eyes.

Shortly after this episode, my mother decided that she was going to leave the country on a raft. She spent several weeks preparing for the trip. The day before our departure, Zacarias's father gave me his address so I could write to them. I never did because life passed, and so did the memory of the boy with honey-colored eyes. I did not suspect such eyes would cross my path only months later.

The morning was passing quietly when I suddenly realized that the guy who was rowing next to me, right in front of me, had stopped. He was a twenty-something-year-old man of black complexion and very stocky. It looked like he exercised a lot. I don't think he was tired. Why will he stop rowing? I asked myself. Suddenly I looked toward the water and saw a white figure under the raft. It was a great white shark, without a doubt. My blood froze. But before I could say anything, the guy signaled me to be quiet. It is said that sharks do not see very well. But they have a sensor that perceives the shadows of an object in the water. They quietly go under boats and rafts until something falls into the water. Tales of the thousands of Cubans eaten by sharks flashed through my mind. But I kept calm as I could. Panic on the raft would have been disastrous.

In my opinion, time passed very slowly, even more so with the latent danger of being devoured by a marine animal or killed by the scorching sun. People had already told us about others who died of dehydration in the hours when the sun hits the most, between 12 and 4 pm. We had spent nearly sixteen hours on the raft when we spotted a helicopter in the sky. I just noticed it was red and white. We all started arguing. Some said it was an American helicopter, others that it was Cuban. The truth is that panic and exhaustion were taking over everyone. For hours the raft had been circling in the same place. I took the compass without knowing how to use it and began ordering them to row on one side for a while to move forward.

After a while, they realized that the raft was advancing, and that was when the helicopter arrived like a ray of hope. A flash of light amid all that blue. After turning around in the sky, the red and white metallic bird disappeared, leaving us in an uncertain desolation.

Everyone kept arguing, and I drifted into the memory of the many fights my mom and stepdad had. Episodes in which coexistence was unbearable. The shouting, the insults. I never got along with that man. I always longed for reconciliation between my parents, although one day, I understood that the twelve years of age difference between my mom and dad was a big obstacle for that to happen. My mother always looked younger, and my father was so white and battered I blamed his bad smoking habit. But in the end, it was my father, the man I admired the most, and all the girls my age. The man who knew everything and who could do everything. I also admired my father's green eyes, which were the only thing I regretted not inheriting from him. Who knows how that idea came to me, but I imagined I would be much more beautiful if my cinnamon skin contrasted with blue-green eyes.

Apparently, the helicopter crew notified their superiors about our existence because shortly after, we saw a huge ship on the horizon. A ship the size of those cruise ships that I had only seen in American movies. It was majestic! From the boat came a raft to pick us up. Two men who came in the boat helped us get on. They helped us with extreme care. I assumed they knew about the sharks staying under the rafts. Just like the one I had seen during the journey, it's good that I kept silent because that would have caused total panic among the people on the raft.

For some reason, they ordered us to take off our shoes. I was very upset about leaving behind the new sneakers that my mom had just bought me. With a lot of effort, she finally saved enough money to buy them. They were purple glitter sneakers that came to my ankle. She had bought them, hoping to arrive in the United States with brand-new shoes. A statue of the virgin of Regla also had to remain on the raft. The idol was about two feet tall and painted in striking colors, and she wore a crown on her head. My mom had brought it on the trip, hoping it would protect us on the way. It hurt her a lot to leave that doll on the raft. I did not understand why she put so much faith into a plaster sculpture.

The small motor raft quickly reached the ship that was to pick us up. I couldn't believe it; I had never been on such an impressive ship. I had never been on a big boat! Other people had also been rescued from that vast desert of water. My mother and I looked at the immensity of the ocean we had left behind. A few tears of joy mixed with the salty seawater.

From the railing of the boat, we saw how our small improvised raft was set on fire to sink it; after a few minutes, it succumbed to the waves of the sea. And at the bottom of that ocean, my brand-new tennis shoes and the virgin of Regla drowned out of existence.

2
THE MOTHERSHIP

THAT SHIP SEEMED TO belong to American sailors, but it led us to a second gray ship that looked like a warship. Years later, I would see boats like this on TV on channels like Discovery. I heard that some called it a "Mothership" and said that planes and helicopters landed there. Upon arrival, we realized that there were many rescued. Sure, hundreds, maybe thousands. Everything was so different. My bulging eyes were wide open to experience this new world. A world that seemed opulent and abundant because they offered us new sandals, bedspreads, and enough food as soon as we stepped on the ship. Food that, with the passing of time, I discovered was baby porridge and oatmeal. But to me, everything seemed exquisite, delicious, and new.

On that ship, I met an American sailor who, for some reason, took a liking to me. Perhaps he would have noticed that I was one of the few people among so many refugees who could speak a few words of English. I had noticed this and bragged to my new ship friends. I barely communicated with the sailor, but he didn't seem to care. He always looked for me so that I would sing, "Ese lunar que tienes cielito lindo junto a la boca, no se lo des a nadie, cielito lindo que a mi me toca"... I didn't understand why he liked that song so much. And despite the fact that Watson knew that I was not Mexican, he expected that I would know it to perfection. I didn't mind singing it a thousand times; I had fun watching him laugh, with a few laughs that showed his perfect white teeth, and at the same time, his beautiful green eyes lit up.

Even though we spent a few days on the boat, perhaps four, a hard-to-define affection arose between us. I liked it when he would come to wake me up in the middle of the night to give me candy or teach me to sing the US Navy song. There I lay stretched out on the quilt they had given us, along with hundreds of refugees who were sleeping on the runway for US Navy planes. We had deep conversations despite my limited English. One day Watson told me about the war, and I asked him what he would do if he were given orders to kill or what would happen if there were children like me in the middle of the conflict. Watson was silent, looking a little sad but determined at the same time.

On the day of the farewell, the sun shone brightly. There was lots of activity at the pier where the Mothership had arrived. When our group got on the bus that would take us to our destination, I noticed tears running down my cheeks. And while looking for the sailor through the window, I saw him on the other side of the pier, and I realized that his green eyes had tears too.

3
THE CAMP

THE BUS TOOK US to a military camp. Full of dark green military tents with dirt floors. There were hundreds of disoriented people who were hungry and wanted to bathe. About two days after being there, they put up a tent with makeshift showers and toilets. Apparently, they did not expect so many people. Much less 30,000 Cubans! They had to divide the group into several camps. Soon we realized that we were not in the United States. We were at the Guantánamo naval base in Cuba.

As the days passed, the camp became a kind of urbanized city. They had put up bathrooms and a dining room that would make the best hospital envious; there was even a small school, a clinic, and a makeshift church. One day my mom took me to the clinic because she didn't know how to deal with the lice that plagued me. My mother had tried all kinds of treatments in Cuba. Many times, I even spread kerosene. That was how I met Geovanny. According to him, I had my head down, sitting on a cot while my mom took the annoying bugs out of my hair. Geovanny was a Cuban guy from Alamar, a barrio in Havana. He had fair skin, black hair, and honey-colored eyes, or hazel, as he said.

I had not noticed him because in those days, I was entertained by a boy my age, also white with golden curls. Despite the fact that we had been in the camp for a few days, that boy had already gone to our tent to ask my mom for my hand in marriage. So, I hadn't really noticed Geovanny. I hadn't noticed him until I started attending those gatherings where people sang or told stories to pass the time. It caught my attention that Geovanny played the guitar and sang just like José José, or so it seemed to me. In their eagerness to entertain people, Geovanny and his friends formed a group called "Aggravated Assault" , what a crazy name for a band, I thought. Geovanny was in his early twenties, and with his charm and voice, he seemed to be the leader of the group. In addition, his hazel eyes mesmerized anyone. Many in the camp spent long hours at night listening to the group sing popular ballads that filled us with joy and nostalgia.

From one day to the next, they announced in the camp that several people had to be transferred to the Panama Canal Base. There were too many people. Many families tired of being in that camp offered to go first. Among those families was mine. I had to say goodbye to the boy with the golden curls. He asked me not to go, but I told him my mom had decided. I would never see him again, although from time to time, I remembered him with nostalgia. Geovanny was also in the group that decided to go to Panama.

The journey to Panama would be by plane. It was the first time I got to fly. Filled with excitement and curiosity, I couldn't believe how beautiful the clouds looked and how small the landscape looked from above. Even though we were not going to the United States, I was happy with the new experiences. I was looking out the window of the plane, open-mouthed from being among the clouds, and simultaneously, I remembered with melancholy everything I had left behind.

4
PANAMA

UPON ARRIVING AT THE Panama Canal camp, I realized that my little brother was very close to Geovanny, and naturally, we became closer. Soon Geovanny and I were walking hand in hand around the camp. It was obvious that he was older than me. He was stocky and average in size compared to my skinny frame. I didn't care at all. I was happy when he took me on the swings, and we swayed in the moonlight while he sang romantic ballads. Besides, I was delighted that an older guy had noticed me. Geovanny gave me a lot of confidence and raised my self-esteem.

One of those nights, after singing and silencing the nostalgia, we went to the tent where Geovanny slept. There was no one, and all the curtains were down. It's as if he had agreed with his friends to leave us alone. In the eternal calm of that night, the rough green canvases of that tent turned into beautiful tulles, and the uncomfortable cot was the finest mattress. Our bodies intertwined. One smaller than the other but with the same size in the dorsal part. Between kisses and passions, he lifted my dress; I reminded him that I had never had sex before, he understood, and we stopped.

As the days and events in the camp continued to pass, I noticed that at night some Cuban women went wrapped only in sheets to where the American soldiers stood guard. The girls had sexual relations with them for boxes of cigarettes or certain privileges like leaving the camp for a couple of hours.

I remembered how in Cuba, on several occasions, my friends had suggested that I go with them to see foreigners at the hotels in the area. My answer was always the same, NO! My clothes were not branded, nor did they have any kind of luxuries, but when I got home, there was always something to eat. My friends were in the same situation. It occurred to me that many had an ambition that clouded their moral compass.

The days went by without realizing that I had already become Geovanny's girlfriend, even though I was only fourteen. In our culture, it was normal, I guess. No one batted an eye to see a teenager with a twenty-something years old guy. I realized I was still a kid when I went to the women's bathroom one day, and in the middle of a group showering women, I felt a warmth between my legs. When I looked down, my legs were covered in blood. There were several women around me in that makeshift shower. I felt a horrible shame; I wanted the earth to swallow me right there. That feeling of humiliation suddenly changed when I realized that what happened was like a ritual that turned me from a girl to a woman. I imagined myself after a short time fully developed. I was finally going to have some enviable curves. But none of that happened, if not many years later.

5
USA vs. CUBA

THE TENSIONS IN THE camp became more and more palpable. Many refugees were desperate to get out of there. Rumors of a revolt began to spread. A few days later, I heard a brawl. People ran from there to here. There were people yelling profanities at the American soldiers on the other side of the fence. The harps of a war helicopter were heard very loud. I left my tent scared and saw that the helicopter was hovering above very close to us. Suddenly, between the tents, a soldier sped up with an SUV coming towards me at full speed. Geovanny had to push me out of the way to avoid getting hit. The scene was total chaos.

The next day the atmosphere was still tense. The Cubans were yelling at the American guards to get us out of that place. I heard that a group of Cubans were throwing stones and cans in protest. I ran to where the commotion was being heard to ensure Geovanny wasn't wrapped up in the fuss. When I got to the place, I saw Geovanny among the people. I started yelling at him, trying to get his attention. Stones, screams, and sticks were flying everywhere. Geovanny ran over to me and led me back to my tent. That night he stayed with us in the family tent, and I could not fall asleep all night.

The next day in the breakfast line, we saw several men with eye patches, bandages in one arm, one leg. When we asked what had happened, they said that the American guards came to the single men's tent at dawn to beat them up for the brawl they had caused. Geovanny was relieved that he hadn't spent the night in his tent. Some found what had happened funny, but I was frightened by the uncertainty of the situation. I felt that if, at any moment, the Cubans became desperate and revolted again, the gringos were going to kill us all.

6
FORBIDDEN GAMES

THE DAYS AND NIGHTS in the camp were long. We were starting to get bored. A group of teenagers would get together at night to tell horror stories. The story of the headless black knight, or the story of the Uijes in Cuba. Legend has it that these Uijes were small, black, ugly creatures living near the rivers. Few people had seen them, legend or not, we were all terrified by the stories.

One of those nights, I don't know how one of the kids got hold of a Ouija board. This game was made famous by a horror movie from the 80s. For many, it is not real, but definitely, behind this game that seems so innocent, there are evil forces that can destroy your life. Without knowing it, many people have made a contract with satan and his demons by participating in this "simple" game.

The board contains all the letters of the alphabet from A to Z. The game also has a plastic heart with a kind of magnifying glass in the center. Two people lightly put their index fingers on the heart so that the heart could slide on the board, indicating the answers letter by letter.

We were four teens, playing two at a time; we passed the board around and asked questions to the mysterious beings from beyond. When it was my turn, I fearfully placed my fingers on the plastic grommet, and my hands began to move rapidly. I asked: How long are we going to be in this camp? The compass started to move and spelt out: FIVE.

7
THE QUINCEAÑERA

EXACTLY FIVE MONTHS LATER, a few months before I turned fifteen, my family was set to leave the camp. For some time in Cuba, my mother had saved money for my quinceañera. Mom had bought some things for my party. The typical bikini, plastic cutlery, and other little things. But there I was in that camp about to celebrate my birthday amid uncertainty, without most of my family, my party clothes, and without cake.

There is a saying in Cuba that says: "Necessity is the mother of invention" . I don't know where a man who made birthday cakes appeared in the camp. They weren't real birthday cakes, though; he made them out of cardboard boxes and shaving cream. Of course, this was just for photographic effects. Mine was beautiful! Who knows how the inventive artist made the pink cream and ended up making a three-tier pink and white cake worthy of any cardboard princess? I also don't know where a camera roll came from, but they took a number of photos with different changes of clothes. All with the desire to please my mother, who had dreamed so much of my fifteenth birthday. There were no gifts except for the one Geovanny gave me.

8
THE GIFT

WHEN EVERYTHING BECAME QUIET, Geovanny took me to his tent. This time the desire and urgency of our passion did not allow arguments, and we both succumbed to our unbridled instincts. That night, between the curtains of military tents and the darkness of the Panamanian night, I lost my virginity.

A few days after our encounter, they told us that my family was finally leaving Guantanamo. It had been exactly five months. It was time to start taking people out in this order. First, families with minor children, single women, couples, the elderly, dogs (some joked) and finally, single men. Many people gathered for that purpose, and others denied their real age. As well as a friend who was about twenty, he lied and said he was fourteen years old; because of his youthful appearance it worked. That's how his family got out faster.

The parting was sad. Perhaps much more for me because I felt that I was leaving in that camp the memory of my first period, my first love encounter and Geovanny. He had to stay since he was on the list of single men. He promised he would come looking for me as soon as he got to the United States.

9
NEW COUNTRY

WE ARRIVED FIRST in Miami. We were placed in a cheap motel in the area for a couple of days. In Panama, Geovanny had given me his aunt's phone number so I could contact her when I got to Miami. The lady agreed to meet with me.

We met at sunset when it was beginning to get dark. He picked me up at the motel entrance and took me to a nearby supermarket. When I entered the grocery store, my mouth fell open. I had never seen such opulence in my life. All the shelves were packed with products. My eyes were wide open, looking for where to land, but it was impossible. There was so much to see, treats, all kinds of breads, meats! The lady smiled and looked at me like someone who saw a child receive his favorite toy. After buying a few items, she took me back to the motel but not before leaving me with the following phrase: "Things in the United States are not as rosy as you have heard in Cuba." Her words sounded cynical but held a grain of truth deep down.

The agency in charge of us was a Catholic charity, and it was a non-profit organization. I heard a rumor that to stay in Miami, we had to have a sponsor, someone who would take responsibility for us. But since we didn't have any relatives in the United States, the agency gave us a couple of options. The man in the office only spoke English, so he hardly communicated with me. The first option was to be sent to Minnesota and the second to New Mexico. I translated for my mom what the representative said. We were not familiar with either location. So, I asked him in my broken English which of the two places was less cold. And smiling, he answered, Albuquerque, New Mexico.

10
NEW MEXICO

NEW MEXICO IS A STATE near Arizona in the desert area. It is known for its annual hot-air balloon festival. The first week of October, the sky is filled with hundreds of balloons of different sizes and colors; it's really a sight to watch. But in the season that we arrived, it was very cold and covered with snow. Since we didn't have a car, my mom would go shopping at the market and come back dragging the metal cart from the supermarket. Our feet were freezing as we only had tennis shoes and not the right boots for the weather.

Why, then, did they call this place the land of enchantment? I always wondered. Someone told me it was one of the few places in the United States where no natural disasters occurred. No earthquakes, tornadoes, or storms to worry about. And with that information little by little, I got used to the idea that the cold and the snow weren't so bad.

In any case, those first weeks in the United States seemed like centuries. I didn't get used to the people, the customs, the food, or the language. Above all, the language, I met reality. In English, I only knew how to say my name, where I was from, and a few wrong conjugated verbs; I wondered how Watson understood me. Together with my mom, we spent several funny moments in stores and restaurants when paying or ordering food.

Besides, I missed Geovanny terribly; I started writing to him every day. I told him about every new thing I discovered, what I felt for him, and covered each letter with kisses, poems, and other corny things. Geovanny sent me a lot of letters, too, only that his poems were much better than mine. I attributed it to his soul as a poet and troubadour. No wonder he sang and wrote such beautiful songs. In such a short time in the camp, I discovered many things about him; I learned about his parents in Cuba and brother who lived in Miami, and his other brother who had passed away, how many sisters he had, nephews, his ex-girlfriend's name, and even details of how he had been unfaithful with his model friends. He told me many things. Perhaps because, despite my scarce fifteen years, I seemed to reason with total maturity. In some ways, I was still a child. Geovanny always criticized my constant running around everywhere. Wherever I went, I ran as if I was running from something. When he complained to me, I always repeated:

"Okay, next time I'll walk." My immature jealousy would also show up occasionally, or I would get mad if he dawdled when I was talking to him. In any case, we came to have a rapport beyond simple physical contact.

11
CONSEQUENCES

It didn't occur to me that the physical contact Geovanny and I had enjoyed would have terrible consequences. What I saw when I looked at myself in the mirror frightened me. The changes in my body were noticeable; I realized that my breasts were getting bigger day by day. Despite my slim figure, my breasts looked huge. I had definitely changed. For a moment, I thought that God had finally heard my prayers to have curves, but the latent doubt of the most likely scenario crept into my mind, could I be pregnant? I wondered; I didn't even want to contemplate the possibility. Several weeks passed before I told my mom that I was feeling unwell. I was pale, didn't want to do anything, and vomited everything I ate.

Perhaps my mom had already noticed it too, but was in total denial, just like me.

Finally, we went to the doctor together. They did the corresponding tests to determine why I was feeling so sick. The cold medical room made matters worse, and I was freezing, not so much from the cold in the room but from the panic that consumed me. I wouldn't know how to deal with my mother's reaction and what explanation to give her. Especially after mom had told me that Geovanny was an older man and wouldn't be willing just to be dating. The air became dense; I looked at the clock as I played with my hands. Suddenly the doctor came in, announcing a positive pregnancy result, and my mother became hysterical. She started screaming, "I can't believe you did this to me!" I have seen this scene in movies and soap operas countlessly, but now I was the main actress, and having nothing to say, I bowed my head.

The days that followed further deteriorated my physical and emotional state. I was getting thinner by the day, with only 89 pounds of flesh and bones. I held nothing in my stomach. No jellies, no cookies; nothing took away my disgust and vomiting. Also, not being with Geovanny deteriorated me emotionally.

One of those days, a neighbor from the apartment where we lived knocked on the door. The door was half open, and when he entered, he saw me stretched out on the sofa as if dying. He called the ambulance, and they took me to the ER. My mom was at work, getting a call, and she got to the emergency room as soon as possible. The doctors announced that I was dehydrated, which was critical to my state of pregnancy. They were recommending an abortion. They said that my fragile body would not withstand childbirth.

A few days later, my mother accompanied me to one of those clinics where babies often pay for the immaturity of their parents. A lady doctor called me privately and consulted me, she asked me if I was clear about what was going to happen. Perhaps the doctor wanted to ensure that I had the maturity to make that decision. But didn't she see that I was only 15 years old?! What could I know? The maturity I had boasted about so many times was now rubbed in my face, making me understand that just having sex does not make you a mature woman. Now was the time to make the most precarious decision of my life. I remembered that one of my cousins in Cuba had done the same thing several times when she was only 13 years old. That day, I would also make this irrevocable decision out of selfishness, confusion, pressure, or fear of dying.

The procedure was relatively quick. I felt a cold metal device open my cervix, and suddenly an instrument that sounded like a vacuum cleaner got rid of the little person inside.

12
MY SIXTEEN BIRTHDAY

BETWEEN GUILT, CONFUSION, JOY, and tears, another birthday arrived. I was turning 16, and Geovanny was still in the Panama camp. I wrote him a letter telling him what had happened with the baby. Geovanny tried to comfort me through his letters. His support, even from a distance, made that moment less difficult.

My birthday arrived, and with the few resources my mother had, we prepared a small party in the apartment that the Catholic agency had paid three months of rent for us. It was an apartment in a neighborhood where crime was the daily bread. Drug deals on street corners and shootings a few doors away were part of the daily scene. A couple of doors from ours, a neighbor took his own life. Nobody knew anything about him, not even his name. The environment made me depressed, and it was totally different from Cuba, where all the neighbors knew each other and treated each other like family.

I remember that the agency also sent us an English tutor so that my brother and I could at least understand the basics to join the school. She was a young, blonde and very nice girl. With what she taught us; we could start school under an ESL (English as a Second Language) program. I started my first year of high school. In that neighborhood, I felt so far away from everything I knew. Far from my family and my friends and far from my father.

13
MY FATHER

AS A CHILD, MY FATHER was my everything. Like any little girl, he was perfect to me. He was really smart. He was very fond of reading and was very knowledgeable about literature, politics and a wide variety of topics. Confirmation of this came one day when I was walking with my father down the street, and a lady with gray hair stopped us. Seeing us, she yelled: Joaquinito! Is it you?! My dad replied: Yes, teacher, it's me. My father, with his blue-green eyes and upturned nose like an eagle, was easy to recognize anywhere. The lady asked what he did for a living. My dad said he was a bricklayer and a carpenter. An air of disappointment covered the teacher's face. And she said: "I thought you were going to be a diplomat with the high qualifications you had. Your father is very smart," she said; we then said our goodbyes, and each one went their way.

My parents met when my mom was 14, and my dad was 12 years older. Since my mom was a minor, my dad would always tell my mom that they had to wait until she turned 18 to start dating. And indeed, when she turned 18, they got married in a beautiful wedding in the newlyweds' palace in Cuba.

Their courtship was not easy. Since dad had a racist grandmother who sneered at my mom when she came to visit him. But my grandparents, that is, my father's parents accepted her as a daughter. So, when my brother and I came into the world, we had two families, one white and the other black. I remember when I was little, they asked me, do you want to go to your grandmother's house? And I innocently would ask: To white grandmother's house or to a black grandmother's house. Although both families were Cuban, they had a different culture. Only my two grandparents and my father's sister lived in the Fortun house. Grandpa had a room full of antique china, gold, silver, and other interesting items. My grandfather would give me earrings or some old porcelain doll when I visited them. When I visited my black side of the family, the López, there was always a party, drinking, fun, and the occasional fight.

My dad always instilled in me the love of reading. He was one of those people who was reading a book while eating or even when he went to the bathroom. He would get very angry when he saw young people on the street wandering around with nothing to do. He always said: Why don't they spend time reading a book, learning something?! My dad had a small bookcase which was his pride and joy. In this small piece of furniture that he had built, there were a lot of literature works, science, and other books. I remember seeing Don Quixote de la Mancha and several books by Truman Capote. Despite his love for reading, I never saw a Bible in my house. I can't even remember my father mentioning it. It is common knowledge that the Bible is the best-selling book throughout history. Looking back, it saddens me that my father, being a skilled reader, would never have read the Bible.

14
THE INITIATION

My mother says that an uncle of hers introduced my father to the occult world. The uncle was called godfather since he was a high-ranking sorcerer. At one of the satanic parties my mom attended, she said that while everyone jumped and danced to the beat of drums, the godfather would put gunpowder on some of the attendees' backs. Gunpowder was poured in the shape of a cross on the backs of them and set on fire. Those who did not scream or did not get burned were said to have "the dead mounted." This is the term used to indicate when an entity possesses someone. They would begin to speak about the occult and secret things, look into the future, and so on. At just fifteen years old, my mother saw with her own eyes how gunpowder did not burn my father; everyone was impressed by this. In easier-to-explain terms, a demon had already possessed him. From that day on, he earned the respect of others and began his training as a witch doctor.

My father became a warlock with "moral ethics", so to speak. I often heard him say, "There are two things I don't do in witchcraft. One is to kill people, and the other is to tie up men to a woman." So, I grew up believing my father was doing something good. I think he only helped people heal from diseases and get out of certain legal troubles. Many neighbors, acquaintances and strangers came to see him to get help with their problems.

I have seen with my own eyes how black magic achieves healing and certain "miracles". I have seen people get out of jail or be healed. But what most people fail to realize is that these favors from the occultic world are to be paid back sooner or later. The devil will always come to collect the favors he has given. There was an instance when my brother and I became seriously ill with a fever; my father performed some rituals which made us quickly recover.

On another occasion, my legs were covered in pimples. My mom was a nurse and had some witchcraft powers, she tried various treatments, medicines, and rituals, but nothing worked. For many months they treated various things, and I continued with those pimples full of pus on my legs. My mother decided that since this case was more serious, we had to go to Santiago de Cuba to make a promise to the Virgin of Regla. The Virgin of Regla's shrine, Santiago de Cuba, is in a province on the island and takes a 12-hour drive from Havana. So, the journey was exhausting and expensive;

but my mom made the trip. After making a promise to the idol, the pimples disappeared when she returned. Thinking back, I understood why my mom had so much faith in this idol and had it accompany us on the raft.

The Virgin of Regla is just one of many idols invented by the Cuban people. Legend has it that three fishermen went out to the sea long ago in a small boat. On their return, the weather turned bad, and the sea was choppy. The waves threatened to sink the fragile boat. The fishermen began to ask for help and suddenly saw the Virgin of the Regla image in the sky. It is said that the Virgin rescued them, and since then, the Virgen de Regla has been more famous than Christ on the island. However, just as the bible says, I realized that there is no other name given to men in which there is salvation. (Acts 4:11-12). So, anything we put our hope in beside God is pure idolatry. And idolatry itself is an abomination to God. (Exodus 20:5)

Unfortunately, culture teaches us something different. And without getting informed, reading or investigating, we do things that our relatives taught us for generations.

15
MY PARENTS SEPARATION

I WAS NINE YEARS old when my parents separated. It was definitely difficult for my brother and me. There was a lot of fighting and shouting. My dad started drinking more than usual, and he would leave us home alone for long periods. One of those nights, he came home drunk and asked me if we had eaten. I told him no. The realization that because he was drinking with his friends, he had forgotten to leave us something to eat turned into rage. Suddenly he began to hit the kitchen counter with fury. And when he felt his fist swell up, he stopped hitting and began to cry. I had never seen my father so sad and miserable.

His constant drunkenness reached such a point that one day he went to fight with some guys from the worst neighborhoods in Havana. The result was that some liquid was poured into his eyes, and he was left blind for several months. During this season, I helped him bathe and fed him. But as soon as he recovered, he returned to the house of those thugs with a friend of his whose nickname was the Gorilla, and they beat everyone in the house. They sent one of the guys to the hospital. When the nurses came out and left the patient alone, my dad and his henchmen would sneak into the room and threaten him. The guy would shake with fear and call for someone to help him. My dad told this story between laughs and an air of having committed a great feat.

During my childhood, I remember that my father spent much time away from home. They told me he was not in the city because he was working in the fields. As I grew older, I heard stories that explained his absence for indefinite periods.

On one occasion, he went out partying and passed out on the way home in a taxi. At dawn, the police arrived and found the taxi driver dead in the front seat with my father drunk in the back. He was accused, but my dad swore that he had not murdered the driver. And with the help of my mother, who was a nurse, they put him in a psychiatric hospital to escape time in prison.

After a month and a half of being hospitalized, he already felt like he was really going crazy. As there were some unusual behaviors from the patient. There was a patient who did not stop marching day and night since he called himself Napoleon Bonaparte. There were piercing screams and deranged people out of their minds. My dad called my mother desperately, and after a lot of paperwork, they let him free. The godfather also did his witchcraft work, so the legal charges were dropped. Another favor the devil was doing him, another favor he would have to pay for later on.

16
SATANIC GATHERINGS

IN THE OCCULT WORLD, it is common to make animal sacrifices. My father's apartment in Lawton, a neighborhood in Havana, had an abandoned terrace where he did all his witchcraft ceremonies. On that terrace, my dad had four-foot-high wooden doors. Behind these doors, an altar was hidden. In this space, the ephod was kept; it is a kind of cauldron with objects of black magic. The word ephod is also in the bible, satan likes to use bible names in his tricks to confuse people. In my dad's cauldron, there were different objects, all made of iron to represent various spiritual jobs. I remember that there was a hammer, a stake, a horseshoe and other objects. Some of the items were rusted or covered in dried blood.

From time to time, several of my father's friends would come and perform rituals on the terrace. After greeting each other: "Ekelecua", They opened the two wooden doors to expose the cauldron, and they began to play the drums, drink rum, and smoke tobacco. After a while, they would kill a chicken, cutting its throat, and while it was still trembling, they all drank from the hole where blood gushed from. The animal's blood was poured over the ephod, giving off a malevolent odor over time. At a young age, I simultaneously looked at this grotesque scene with disgust but curiosity and interest. What are they doing all this for? I was wondering. At the end of the ceremony, my father would put a black cloth over the ephod. Once, I asked dad: why do you do that, why do you cover it? And he told me: "That rag is placed over the cauldron so that God does not see what we are doing." That was the first indication I had that my dad knew what he was doing was wrong. How innocent can we be, nothing and no one hides from God.

At other times they hung a lamb from a tree by its front legs by a rope. They'd slit his throat, and while the blood flowed, the little animal just looked with eyes that were too sad to describe. I heard my dad say several times that the lamb was the only animal he was sorry to kill because it looked at you with eyes that seemed human.

From time to time, we went to these satanic gatherings, which lasted almost until sunrise. Upon entering there, we were always met with several altars, each color representing a saint, red for chango, blue for yemaya, etc. The altars were full of fruits, money, honey and other offerings. Many people came, and everyone brought something to offer on the altar.

At around midnight, between the drinking and the drums, someone was mounted by "the dead". That person would go into a trance, speak in a deep, strange voice, and move erratically. Today I know that these were demons that possessed those people. At that moment, I was only amazed to see how this person began to speak and guess things about the lives of the attendees. On one occasion, the possessed guy went to one of the ladies present and revealed that she was cheating on her husband; as you can imagine, drama ensued.

17
MY BROTHER'S INITIATION

IN THOSE DAYS, I began to inquire more about the spiritual. My fascination for knowing where we came from and where we were going began to grow. I started attending a Catholic church where they taught catechism classes to the neighborhood's children. I told my dad I was going to church, and I liked what I heard and invited him to go with me; with a tender voice, he answered: "I can't go, but pray for me."

I often heard my father say I would be the first woman to be part of his "Palo". Which meant I was going to be the first woman to be initiated into his satanic cult. Each "Babalawo" or sorcerer has his own clan of people who have been baptized, so to speak, in his group.

My brother's satanic initiation was a great event for my father. At seven, my brother was put through a dedication ritual. With a razor blade, they made a couple of cuts in the shape of an upside down cross on his small chest. The godfather who had initiated my father said that my brother was the son of a chango (one of the many deities of the folklore of Yoruba religion). Through this ritual, he was supposed to be protected by him. After throwing some snails on the floor, along with some chains, the name of the new member of the clan was revealed. Followed by hours of drumming where more evil forces were invoked over my poor little brother's life.

18
NIGHTMARES

ALL THE DOORS MY father opened to the devil began to affect us. During my childhood I started having nightmares almost every night. I rarely remember sleeping peacefully. I felt as if a black cloak covered me and squeezed me simultaneously, to the point of not being able to move or wake up. It was a terrifying experience that I went through constantly.

Other times during the night, I had dreams of a tall, white man with brown hair, wearing an impeccable black suit with a tie of the same color. He would appear in my dream and, on several occasions, had intimacy with me, despite the fact that I was a girl of barely eight years old. This dream man looked to be around twenty-eight years old. I later realized that these demons came to torment me at night due to the many occultic things my father was involved in. This last demon later on I understood was what we call in deliverance a "spiritual husband". It is a demon that satan assigns to one's life to cause marriage failure; it's like being spiritually married to the devil. That is why it is very dangerous to have sex with someone who appears to you in dreams; they are demons making contracts with you. All these spiritual ties I had to break through prayers later on.

19
MANTILLA

AFTER MY PARENTS SEPARATED, my mom moved to Mantilla, a neighborhood on the outskirts of Havana. It was a seedy neighborhood with a high crime rate and many people with a low reputation. We were welcomed into the neighborhood with my brother and I being beaten up by some kids from a very sketchy family. Feared by many neighbors, this family was known as: "the meat monkeys". Mom left us alone in the house to go to work at the hospital; the neighborhood's children knew that we were left alone, so they did everything possible to intimidate us. The first week my brother and I were terrified because they would stand outside the house with sticks and stones and threaten to hurt us if we dared to go outside. After the first week, I told my brother: "We are not going to let them exile us." A slang phrase meant they would never let us out of the house. "We have to face them; otherwise, we will never be able to get out of the house." My brother hesitantly nodded, and we headed for the door. That day we took a beating from "monkey meat children." That was our initiation into the neighborhood.

The next day we were all playing as if nothing had happened. I had a split lip, but that didn't stop me from having a smile on my face for having the courage to overcome my fears.

20
OLD HAVANA

AFTER A WHILE, MY mother traded that house in Mantilla for the small room in Old Havana. As I said before the building was super old, and we had to share a small dirty bathroom with the rest of the neighbors. The neighbors took turns cleaning the bathroom. Each family was assigned one day of the week to clean the bathroom. But the toilet and the floor were so old that the smell was putrid no matter how much you cleaned it. Also, the bathroom had no ceiling and was super uncomfortable to use. Often my brother would lie about being afraid that someone could watch him take a shower, so he would go days without touching a drop of water.

The studio was also very small, about the size of a small living room and an upper area where the only bed was. In Cuba, the room made on a studio's roof is called a barbacoa. After going up the makeshift wooden stairs, you went up to the barbacoa, but you couldn't stand up straight because the ceiling was very low. There was only space for a small bed and a TV.

In the afternoons, my brother and I would go to the Plaza. This was the busiest place in the city for tourists. Whenever I saw a tourist, I'd think: "They dress so funny, but they smell so good." They all seemed to be wearing the same uniform, shorts, sandals, a floral shirt, a fishing hat, and a camera around their necks. My mother would tell me: "I don't want you in the square asking tourists for money." My mother, being a nurse, earned very little. A nurse in Cuba at the time only earned about $20 a month. I saw how my mom worked so hard and spent everything on food and essentials. So, I began to imitate my friends; we would meet in the square and begin to hustle tourists: "Friend, friend! Do you have a dollar? Many tourists passed by, but from time to time, someone would pass by and give us some coins. The first time they gave me a dollar, I felt like I had won the lottery. I had never held an American dollar in my hands. I ran out of joy straight for the house. When I got home, my mom was on the barbacoa stairs, I told her hesitantly. "Mom, don't be mad, but I brought you something." I extended my hand, hiding the bill folded in three parts and said: "Here". My mother was surprised. Maybe she had never seen a dollar herself, either. She asked me where I had gotten it from, and I told her they had given it to me at the Plaza. She said, "Thank you very much", and never reproached me again for going to the square. At that time, I was about 12 years old.

21
THE THIEF

ONE DAY A DARK, fat man with thick eyelids that gave his eyes a toad-like appearance came to our apartment in Old Havana. My mom said that man was my grandfather, her father. He definitely hadn't raised her because I had never heard her talk about him before. For some reason, he came to stay with us for a while. With him was his wife, a tall lady, also black. She always tied her hair back, and there was an air of submissiveness about her.

Little by little, the couple gained my trust. They were very nice to me and my brother. I already loved them like my long-lost grandparents. One day the wife said she was going out of town. That night my grandfather, brother, and I were in the upper room watching a movie. My little brother had fallen asleep on the bed, and I was awake next to grandpa. Suddenly I felt how his grotesque hand grabbed my small and undeveloped chest. Then he took my right hand and put it over his briefs. I jumped up and went downstairs, where my mom and stepfather were sleeping. I told my mom I wanted to sleep with her because I was scared.

The next morning, I didn't know how to react; thousands of thoughts flooded my head. I knew that what had happened was not right. I decided to tell my mom about what had transpired. When my mom returned from work, I told her what had happened, and she just fell silent and began to cry.

I let a couple of days go by to see if my mom would say something to her so-called father, but that didn't happen. In the meantime, his wife returned from her trip, and when she saw my attitude change toward my grandfather, she asked me: Is something wrong?; erratically, I yelled at her: "Ask your husband what's wrong with me!"

Rage seized me while pondering on the audacity of this man. In the afternoon, when I saw him in the room, I told him defiantly: "You old pig, if you touch me again, I'll tell the whole world!" That same afternoon they packed up their things and left.

Until then, I was a calm and obedient girl. But from that day, a spirit of rebellion entered me. I became a brash and angry teenager. Most of my neighbors hated me as I became very rebellious and disrespectful. All these memories from my past flooded my mind. Meeting Geovanny at the Panama camp brought a bit of peace and stability into my life.

22
FINALLY

GEOVANNY WAS ABOUT TO leave the camp; he sent me a letter; I counted the days with great anticipation. Until one day, the phone rang, and it was his voice: "Hello, I'm here." I felt my heart skip a beat. I had waited so long for this moment. He was calling from Kentucky, the government had sent him there. It had been almost a full year since he arrived at Guantanamo.

A few days later, he was at my apartment's door. I was sixteen years old when we decided to get married. Geovanny asked my mom for my hand in marriage. Since in the United States, the age of majority is 18, my mother had to go to court and sign that she agreed to the union.

We moved to a small apartment in the area. I stayed at home while Geovanny went to work.

The pressures of being in a new country began to affect our relationship. In addition, the age difference also had its effect. Geovanny began to lie and even get involved with very sketchy people. At this time I had gotten pregnant again.

A number of things happened that turned things sour. But the last straw that broke the camel's back was the night when Geovanny did not come back home from work. I waited a couple of hours for him to return before phoning a friend; I was pregnant with our first daughter at that time. I called my friend to tell her about my worry; while conversing, she suggested I check the closet, and she was right; there was none of his clothing in the closet. At that moment, the world came crashing down on me. What would I do at only sixteen years old, pregnant, jobless, and alone? I hung up the phone and began to cry uncontrollably.

A few days later, Geovanny called from Miami. He was sorry for what he had done and wanted to come home. As I found out later, he had gotten involved with some drug dealers in the city and, with some money that he swindled from them, had escaped to Miami. Soon after that call, the drug dealers followed my car one day after school. I was very scared and told my mom to get to my apartment immediately. I told my mom what had happened, and with great certainty, she said: "Let's go talk to them". I was terrified and didn't want to go talk to those guys. Based on the description I gave my mother; she knew who they were; they were also Cuban. Back then, there weren't many Cubans in the city, and it was easy to tell who was who. We arrived at some sketchy apartments in the roughest part of Albuquerque. We went up to the second floor, and my mother knocked on the door. A dubious-looking black man opened for us.

After exchanging greetings, we walked into the apartment, and my mother asked: Do you know who my daughter is? They said no. My mother, with a super convinced attitude, said: Well, she is Eagle's daughter! The Eagle was my dad's street name in Cuba due to the huge eagle tattoo he had on his chest. Instantly the men got a little nervous and apologized. Wow! I had no idea that my dad's criminal reputation had an effect even in the United States. With a triumphant air, we said goodbye and never heard from them again. Thinking about it, I now recognize that those criminals were more afraid that my father was a famous warlock and could do witchcraft on them. In Cuba, sorcerers have a lot of influence in the community. A "Babalawo", a high-level sorcerer, can end a person's life if he chooses to. Which is a very dangerous thing; the devil uses them as puppets in the destruction of other people and themselves. Only the blood of Jesus covers you as a Christian from this type of evil lurking around us.

A lot happened between Geovanny and me, but that betrayal was the most disappointing thing he ever did to me. I never got over it. I no longer trusted him; and after two years of turmoil I decided to leave him forever. Once again the parting was sad, this time we knew it was forever. We were both sitting in his car, and between tears and dismissals, we said our goodbyes. By then, I had already turned eighteen years old, and we already had two little girls, so it was best to stay on good terms.

23
THE BOY FROM THE CLUB

AFTER SEPARATING FROM GEOVANNY, I tried to curtail my sadness by going out with friends to the club. Since Albuquerque was a small city, there was only one Latino nightclub in the entire city. Wearing my best clothes, I went to the disco with an English name we couldn't pronounce. The place was dark, but you could see that it was something like an Old West-style diner. The music boomed with Salsa and Merengue. I was leaning against a wall when a short boy with a cinnamon complexion approached me. As soon as he opened his mouth, I knew he was Cuban. That accent doesn't come off easily. He said his name was Andres.

By then, I had already moved into a low-cost apartment. The rent was very cheap, and I had enough space for my two daughters. At that time, the song "Flies in the house" by Shakira was the biggest hit. I would dance and sweep, feeling sorry for myself, while I cleaned and organized the entire department. Andrés called me all the time to make himself useful. Sometimes he would take me in his car to run errands or other chores. Next thing you know, something was growing between us, and we began a relationship. I soon learned that he had a daughter with a New Mexican lady. They had separated; who knows why. I couldn't judge him since I was in the same situation; single and with two little girls.

Inevitably, Andrés's ex began to interfere in our relationship. They argued because every time his daughter stayed with us, she had behavior problems. It was clear that the mother would tell her things about me, and she obviously acted out when she was around me. On one occasion, his Ex called the police, and they came over to my house. After talking with the officer, he told me: "You seem to be a decent girl; the best thing you can do is leave that guy alone" he was absolutely right.

On this day, I decided to pay a surprise visit to Andrés in his apartment. I hurried down the corridor until I reached his apartment door. Since the door was ajar, I pushed it and saw that he was talking to his ex. She had her daughter in her arms, and when she saw me, she took after me, enraged. I headed towards the parking lot to avoid trouble. She followed me with her daughter in her arms to the parking lot. She began to insult me and was yelling all kinds of obscenities. The next words that came out of my mouth were: "Let go of your child, and I'll show you!" As soon as she put her daughter on the floor, I jumped on her without noticing two things. One, I was wearing my karate uniform since I had just come from my class and two, a police car was parked in the same parking lot. As quickly as the fight started, so quickly did it end. Suddenly I felt the hands of an officer grabbing me off of her and throwing me to the ground. With his knee on my back, he kept yelling. Be still! Be quiet!

They took both of us to the police station. After the paperwork, they took me to a room where a female officer groped me up and down to ensure I didn't have a weapon. As I was on my period, when checking the crotch, the female officer felt something. I explained to her that I was on my days of the month, but she asked me to show her the pad anyway. It was such a humiliating experience; I had never been in a situation like this. Then they took me to one of the offices where two officers were chatting. One of the officers was sitting down; the other had a file in his hand walking around and couldn't stop laughing. I asked him angrily: Why are you laughing? To which he replied: I can't believe that you are 5 '4 weighing 105 pounds, and the other girl is 5' 7 with 120 pounds, and you left her face looking like that. I had a smirk on my face, showing pride and anger at the same time.

They asked me questions about my karate uniform, and I clarified that I had not used martial arts against my opponent. It was clear that I had not used martial arts because the girl's face showed a very deep scratch from the bottom of her left eye to where her lip began. In the United States, it is a crime to use martial arts against someone unless it is for self-defense. After the interrogation, they put me in a cell with several women. The cell was small, and there were about eight or ten women. The room smelled very bad like they hadn't bathed in days. I vowed never to set foot in a place like that again. Since I did not have any type of criminal record, after a few hours, they released me with the promise of appearing in court.

The day of the trial came, and the case came up very quickly. The judge confirmed that I had never been in trouble with the law and was a good student. So, my punishment was to do community work for two months. Community work consisted of picking up the garbage accumulated on the city's highways. They would take us there in a city van, give us a fluorescent orange vest and a garbage bag, and we would pick up everything that was left on the side of the road.

24
LOS ANGELES

AT THE AGE OF 21, I decided to leave Albuquerque. I was determined not to go back to Geovanny. And my new boyfriend, Andrés, was still entangled in drama with his ex. I rented a moving van, loaded all my stuff up with the help of my mom and brother, and headed to Los Angeles with my two little girls. My mom was crying, and I saw how she left that part of my story behind through the rearview mirror. Or so I thought.

In Los Angeles, I rented an inexpensive apartment near the University where I was going to attend. I planned to keep going to college while dabbling and trying my hand at modeling and acting. A few days after being in Los Angeles, I called Geovanny to send me money for the girls. He refused to send me money. He told me I was on my own, and questioned why I had moved over there. I felt powerless and angry to the point that tears flowed down my cheeks. I was willing and determined to show him that I could make it in LA.

A few days later, I went to a store where I got a prepaid phone and went to an employment agency. After taking the entrance exam, the agency determined that I could work in a law office as a receptionist due to my qualifications.

25
SKYSCRAPERS

THE ELEVATOR TOOK ME to the 11th floor of one of the tallest buildings in downtown Los Angeles. I was nervous, but I felt I was capable of doing the job. The position was that of a bilingual receptionist in a law office Latino attorneys. "Santos y Rodríguez". It sounded very good. I met Mr. Santos, Mr. Rodríguez and the only female lawyer in the firm. Mr. Santos was short but well-dressed and good looking. He had a pretty wife too, but she was a bit stuck up. They both had a little girl of about six years old.

A few weeks after I moved to Los Angeles, Andrés followed me. He said things were going to be better now since his ex was in another state. I agreed to his demand, and we started living together again.

It was already December, and with the festive season came more expenses. Due to so many bills, rent, child care payments, food, gas and so on, I had stopped paying for my car. And they were about to take it from me. I didn't know what to do. This was my only means of transportation. I could not imagine having to ride with my two little girls in the dangerous city buses. The payment due was about $500. I had only been working in the office for a few weeks, so I wasn't expecting the end-of-the-year bonus. But to my surprise, my boss had written me a check. The amount was $500!! Just what I needed to pay for my car. That day I felt that God had done a miracle in my life. On my way home, just about to get on the elevator, my boss stopped the door for me and said: "Money is overrated, Ivet". I answered: "Yes, but not for those who need it". Years later, I realized that he was right. Money is nothing more than an obstacle if we do not have God in our life.

26
DELIVERY GUY

THE DAYS IN THE office were long and full of tension. From time to time, very angry people called, threatening some of the attorneys. In addition, one of the firm's lawyers treated me dismissively and complained about my English accent when answering the phones. Later I found out that he did not like me because his ex-girlfriend had the same name as me. Among all the stress, the highlight of the day was seeing the boy who delivered packages come through the door. He was a tall, slender guy with a mulatto complexion and an angelic smile.

Little by little, we began to establish a friendship. He told me that he was from Nicaragua and had been in the United States for a short time. The guy knew I had a partner, but that didn't stop us from flirting. Every time he came to deliver a package, we struck up a conversation until one day, we exchanged phone numbers.

Soon after, Andrés decided that he was going to Cuba to visit his family. The trip would last more or less a month and a half. A few weeks after his departure, boredom was beginning to overwhelm me. So, I decided to invite the delivery guy over. We were just going to have a "friendly" chat, or so he said. When I put my girls to sleep, I called him and said he could come over. We sat on the couch to talk, and in the middle of the conversation, he jumped on me and tried to kiss me; I was startled and reacted by slapping him. I guess he was just as confused as I was. For men, an invitation to talk can insinuate something else. That was the end of the night. He was embarrassed and so confused. I opened the door for him, and he left.

When Andrés returned from Cuba, I told him what had happened. Deep down, my intentions to tell him were merely egocentric. I wanted him to see that there were other men interested in me. In my mind, I excused myself that I had told him so as not to hide anything from my partner. His reaction was predictable; he became furious and began to insult me. Why did you invite that guy over to the house?! You're just such and such! he kept shouting. The shouting match began escalating, and the next thing I felt was his open hand slapping my face.

At that moment, a sudden memory came to my mind: When I was a teenager in Cuba, one of my aunts told me: "Ivet, you are very daring, and you are very opinionated; when you grow up, you are going to find a man who is going to put you in your place." I answered her: "No man has been born to lay a hand on me!" The memory of my aunt's voice echoed in my mind. I went wild. Andrés, seeing my reaction, twisted my arms forcefully and held me from behind. "Let go of me; you're hurting me," I yelled at him. He wouldn't let go. Since I didn't have my hands free to defend myself, I head-butted him on the nose so hard that he had to let go. I grabbed a ceramic angel on top of the TV set to hit him with it. Apparently, the blow to the nose had been so strong that drops of blood began to fall all over the room while I yelled at him: You're leaving! Else someone is not going to get out of here alive! Andrés packed his things and left at that same hour.

27
HOLLYWOOD

THOSE YEARS IN LOS Angeles are a bundle of memories, most of them not very pleasant. Little by little, I became involved with the Hollywood scene. I signed up with an agency that booked me plenty of extra jobs. An extra is a non-speaking actor part of a movie scene. Something like a human piece of furniture. I always joked about this comparison. The extras give sight and color to what is happening in the filming. It was an easy job, but long hours. The best thing to me was the food they gave us. We would arrive at the set very early, between 5:30 and 6 in the morning, to have breakfast. Breakfast usually consisted of an omelet made on-site by one of the many catering companies out in Hollywood.

The breakfast consisted of fruits, orange juices, porridge, boiled eggs, and yogurts, every good food one could wish for. Then I would go to the makeup and wardrobe trailer, and they would put me in clothes according to my character. Almost always "sexy girl" or passerby. After filming a couple of scenes repeatedly, we went for lunch. Just as delicious as breakfast, lunchtime consisted of chicken, meat, mashed potatoes and some delicious vegetables, all very nutritious. To tell the truth, many were not interested in acting, they were only there for the pay and food; this I found out in between scenes and conversations with other extras. On my days off, I took acting classes and auditioned for movies.

I always liked dancing, so my thing was going from club to club or making music videos. The good thing was that I did not like to drink alcoholic beverages. Whenever I was offered alcohol, memories of my drunken father losing his temper would come to mind. My father was a friendly and funny man, but when he consumed alcohol, he was the angriest and scariest person I have seen to this day. On one occasion, I remember seeing how, in the middle of the street, one of his "enemies" from the neighborhood came to confront him, and my dad grabbed the glass of rum he was holding and smashed it in his face. The man stayed there in the corner crying, and my dad looked at him with pity and told him: "Give a silver bridge to the enemy who cries." That made me understand why many people in the neighborhood were afraid of my father. His fiery temper paired with his fame as a warlock was intimidating for so many in the neighborhood.

My thing was music and dancing. I always resisted alcohol and drugs. But the music of the world also has an intoxicating effect; little by little, I sank into that dark world without realizing it. The years in Hollywood passed quickly; between classes at the university, modeling and acting jobs, time went on.

28
YET ANOTHER BOY FROM THE CLUB

WHENEVER I HAD A problem, my solution was to take refuge at the club. And this time, after having yet another fight with Andrés, was no exception. I was determined never to go back to him again. The very next night, I went to a famous Latin club on the outskirts of East Los Angeles. The club was full, as always. That night, like so many others, I was alone. My addiction to dancing was so great that my friends didn't even want to accompany me anymore. Suddenly a tall, white, black-haired man came up to talk: Are you the girl that appeared on that television show? I didn't know what to answer because I didn't remember which television show he was referring to. I nodded my head in agreement. Turns out he had seen me on a dating show. The guy I dated on the show was Andrés, my real boyfriend, but I hid this detail from the new guy. I thought: Andrés is going to be part of my past; what does it matter?

We spent the whole night dancing, and he couldn't believe he was with the girl he'd seen on TV that week. I thought he was a noble and easy-going guy, although his physique did not appeal to me much. I learned that he was from El Salvador and came from a semi-affluent family. His mom was a lawyer, and his dad was a teacher. They even had a maid who cooked, cleaned and did other chores for them. But here in the United States, he was selling shoes in a store and lived in a house, sharing rent with five other guys.

Few days after meeting Andy, I received a call from Andrés asking me to forgive him. His apologies sounded sincere, but there was definitely not going to be reconciliation. I couldn't let him off the hook because of that slap. I happily told him I had already met someone else and to leave me alone. And just like that, four years of relationship ended. Our courtship was always full of drama, arguments, and complications. So, I decided it was time to jump ship.

29
"FINALLY, I CHOSE WELL"

WE WERE DATING FOR a couple of weeks when Andy confessed to me that he was an illegal immigrant; I felt sorry for his situation and was sympathetic to his struggle.

As the relationship was growing very quickly, I decided to introduce Andy to my little girls. We met in a park. They accepted him immediately, and from that day on, we seemed to be inseparable. We went to the mall, the park, to get ice cream. I was happy to see that my girls loved him and got along with him.

Just a few weeks after we met, a month to be exact, Andy proposed to me. That day I was angry because he was late to pick me up from work. When I got in the car, as I was reproaching him for picking me up late, I was stunned to see that he pulled out a ring. It was a simple ring, but I knew he had bought it with much effort. I immediately said yes.

The day of the wedding came, the ceremony was going to be small, with less than ten people in attendance at one of those many quick wedding venues in downtown Los Angeles. At the time the ceremony was supposed to start, Andy was nowhere to be found. The minister was asking about the groom, and I didn't know what to say. I dialed his cell phone and got no answer. Did he get cold feet? I wondered. Twenty minutes had passed, and I was about to leave when Andy came rushing in. Between apologies and gasps of air, he explained that his friend had come to pick him up late. The minister mentioned various Bible verses and invited us to exchange rings after our vows. I already had the engagement ring that Andy had given me. These new wedding rings came with the ceremony package. They were very simple, the kind that turns your finger green when you sweat. But we couldn't afford anything more.

The photo shoot was in a beautiful local park where there were ducks swimming by and swan boats for rent. I was wearing a pink dress that I had in my closet, and Andy was wearing a black suit that he had rented for the occasion. After the ceremony, we went to the apartment that Andy shared with his friends for the party. It was a home party, with no more than ten people. Mostly Andy's friends and a couple of my friends. My daughters weren't present since they had gone to New Mexico to spend the summer with their dad.

30
TV

ONE DAY ANDY CALLED me very upset. He had been fired from his job. I burst out laughing and said: And why are you crying? You sell shoes! I instantly realized my comment's rudeness, but I had already said it. I began to encourage him by telling him to know he could dedicate his time to what he liked, Radio and Television. Truth be told, he had a voice for the media. Within a few months, he was already working as an intern at a small television station. He wasn't getting paid as an intern, and about six months into the job, he told me: "I'm going to quit my job." I knew he felt bad because he was not contributing financially to the house. I insisted that he not do it, that it was important to go after his dreams and that the process was part of paying "floor rights." During those six months, he had several obstacles. The worst was one of his co-workers. One of the anchors looked down on him and treated him badly. The guy was very arrogant, and in his position as editor and intern, Andy chose to put up with it.

After a while, the sacrifice had its reward. They hired him for a local television station. The station is, to this day, nationally recognized, with branches in every state in the nation. This time they hired him as a producer.

31
REGGAETON

ANDY REALLY LIKED REGGAETON. In the United States, it was just beginning to become very popular. I remembered a dream I had when I was at the camp at Guantánamo naval base. I was on a big stage. In front of me, thousands of people were waiting for me to come out. Suddenly I began to approach the microphone that was on the platform. People applauded, and that's when I woke up. My interpretation of this dream was: "God wants me to be a singer!" So, at the age of twenty-four, I started to get involved in the Reggaeton scene. Consequently, there were tons of parties, trips to the Latin Grammys, escapades to Miami, Las Vegas, and many other cities1

The new trendy beat started to become my obsession. I started writing songs and going to the clubs where Reggaeton was played the most. In a few weeks, I already had more than ten songs. Reggaeton is not a genre where you have to be a poet to write songs, so it was pretty easy for me to come up with new lyrics. With most of the songs ready, I was ready to record an album. Most of the themes in my songs were about female domination and how we didn't need men to be empowered. The theme of female empowerment was what the few female artists of the urban genre rapped on.

In my mind, I imagined what my music videos were going to be like. The speech I would recite when I won my first award, and what color dress I would wear on stage.

32
THE PRODUCER

WHILE I WAS LOOKING for someone to record my first album, someone recommended me to a producer who lived on the outskirts of Los Angeles. The said producer had been married to a renowned Latin singer. But after a bitter divorce, he now lived far from the city and away from his young daughters. After many recording sessions, a feeling began to emerge between us. Long hours in the studio gave space for affection and trust. As they say in Cuba: closeness gives birth to love.

On one of those recording nights, he carried me by the waist and held me against the wall. My legs automatically hugged his waist, and when we were about to kiss, I pushed him. I let go of him, and we both recognized that we were going to make a serious mistake. From that moment, things began to change. We argued about anything and everything. It seemed the physical and emotional tension between us was like a bomb waiting to go off.

Things ended very badly between the two of us. It all culminated in a series of darkly toned and threatening emails. In the end, we decided that for $5,000, he would give me the master and all rights to the album recording.

33
THE PHOTOGRAPHER

ON THE OUTSKIRTS OF the city of Pasadena lived a European photographer. The guy was a bit crazy and bad-mouthed, but I found him interesting since he took very good photos and played the piano. His style of photography was "boudoir", that is, sessions in lingerie and underwear. We did a couple of photo shoots and started hanging out more often. We would go out for coffee or dinner at some of the trendy restaurants around town. Other times we stayed up late in his photography studio while we shared stories from the past or he played the piano. He had other friends who were professional pianists, and they played so well that we would sometimes go to their recitals. I felt like an intellectual interacting with classical music musicians and bowtie events. But the reality was that I was fooling myself. I was just a trophy that accompanied the photographer to those events. The pretty girl who gives the man she accompanies the credibility of a gallant. I always tried for them to see me as more than an object; I wanted them to see my intellectual capacity. But it's like asking a pig to see its food as a beautiful bunch of pearls. Matthew 7:6 says something more or less like this about it.

Our convenient friendship ended the day he yelled at me in the parking lot of his photographic studio: Ivet, F**k You! You just keep flirting with me, and nothing ever happens! Hearing his words made me so angry that I got in my car and decided never to speak to him again. It was very naive of me to think that a real friendship could develop between us in such an environment. Eventually, it is a very dangerous game to play while you are married. I wasn't innocent either, and I knew what I was doing. Flirting gave me an indescribable high. Despite the fact that he sought me out a couple of times to apologize, I never spoke to him again.

34
THE FILM DIRECTOR

IT IS NOT A myth that in Hollywood, many rise to stardom by doing the "casting couch". It's the term used to say that you got a role by sleeping with someone important in the industry. I always heard that this was the rule and not the exception, so when the proposal came to me, it didn't take me by surprise.

They had hired me to play an extra in this movie. The director was digging my look, so he asked me to talk about the possibility of having a better role in his film. I gladly agreed, but I already knew where things were going, so I proposed to meet him at a public place. We eventually met at a restaurant around noon and talked for a while.

He soon realized that he was only going to waste his time with me. If I had never discredited my dignity in Cuba by sleeping with tourists, much less was I going to do it in Hollywood. I have an aunt who told me once: "Ivet, the thing is that you were not born to be a prostitute." The aunt said it with more flowery language, but what she said always stuck with me.

For the second date, he already got a little more daring. He asked me directly if I wanted to be his girlfriend. Which I thought was completely ridiculous since we had hardly known each other. The same simulated and well-worn question I was sure he had told many girls before. I replied that it was not possible because I already had a partner. Between false promises that he was going to give me a better role, the recording of the film came to an end.

For the preview, the director invited dozens of friends and co-workers to his house to watch it. Well, we didn't go to his house directly, but to the conference room located in the gated community where he lived. The place was in one of the best neighborhoods in Los Angeles. One of those places where there is a guard at the gate who asks if your name is on the list. After the premiere in your residence, there was another premiere, this time in a Hollywood theater. There were many people in attendance; since they were presenting the film to see if any distribution company would buy it. The movie itself was impressive. The story gripped you and held your attention from start to finish. But no one ended up buying it.

35
LOVE ADDICTION

I BEGAN TO REALIZE that something was very wrong with me. I constantly craved male attention. It was no longer a choice but a necessity. I needed to hear compliments; I needed to be looked at, to be the center of attention. Those flirtations put me in very uncomfortable and even dangerous situations. By the time I decided to seek help, it was already too late. My marriage with Andy was in shambles.

Since my world was self-improvement, I decided to find more information about what was happening to me. In the process, I discovered a book called Love addiction. In the book, the author explained how this pathology led many people to become addicted to the attention of others. And the level of despair that is felt when the person you are interested in does not give us the attention you think you deserve. It fitted my description exactly, and I always felt incomplete if I wasn't being followed or admired by a man. When God is not the center of our lives, we always take refuge in other things. Whether food, alcohol, drugs, partying, or even other people. Things, in the end, will lead us to a life of misery and loneliness, even when we are surrounded by people or have all the money or attention in the world.

Switching activities, I kept taking refuge in music and clubs. Many times, I would go alone and return home very late. I danced all night with strange men, and in my confused mind, I'd convinced myself that I wasn't doing anything wrong, "I'm just dancing".

Andy, my husband, didn't seem to mind much either, giving me more freedom to continue living my life my way. By then, Andy was working long hours as a television anchor and was busy with his own issues. I'd pick up my girls from school, feed them and put them to sleep, and I wandered off when Andy came home at night.

On one occasion, while I went out of town, someone called Andy to tell him that they had seen me dancing with a guy in a nightclub in Miami. But he already knew that I would be there, so we both laughed at the person who went to him with the gossip. Now I think it was like a self-defense mechanism that helped him deal with something he had no control over.

36
LAS VEGAS

LIKE EVERY YEAR, I was preparing to go to the main Latin show Awards; I headed with a couple of friends to our hotel after the event. We were going through the casino of one of the hotels, and a few steps from the door, a guy from one of the big record labels for the Latino market recognized me. In my opinion, we were friends, and he was trustworthy since I had already stayed at his house in Miami on one occasion, and nothing happened. He asked me where I was going and very kindly told me: If you want, stay upstairs in my room, I won't go up until morning. My friends decided to go to our hotel, and I agreed to stay in his room because the heels I was wearing were killing me. When I got to the room, I took a shower and decided I didn't want to go to sleep with the puffy party dress I was wearing. So, I grabbed a white T-shirt, and some new briefs from a package, put them on and went to bed.

It was early morning when I woke up to the sensation of someone caressing me. As I opened my eyes, I realized that this guy was naked next to me, trying to fondle me. I yelled at him: What are you doing?! Between stammering, he began to ask why I didn't want to be with him. I jumped out of bed. I put on the dress as best I could while he kept begging me not to get angry.

I was angry, confused, and felt like a fool. I went down to the hotel lobby, and from there, I called Andy and told him what had happened. Through tears, I tried to explain how I had ended up in this man's room. He seemed irritated and, at the same time, tired of listening to my many blunders.

37
NEW AGE

TIME IN LOS ANGELES passed. I was still in college and living in a rented house in East Los Angeles. At that time, I was exploring many things regarding spirituality. I remember that everything that was New Age was becoming very popular. There was a book in particular that became a bestseller. Many videos on YouTube began to emerge regarding the topic. This intriguing book promises to give you the secret of how to get everything you could ever want, money, fame, and fortune. Just by using "the law of attraction", all your wishes would come true. Of course, with a promise like that, I had to read that book. I got it at one of the most famous bookstores in the city. One of those libraries that smell like coffee and make you get lost for hours. I devoured the book in a couple of days. I have always been a fast reader, which I learned from my father. I immediately put into practice all the tricks that the book proposed. I began to visualize the things I wanted intensely. I talked to the universe and even made a box of dreams. The book also mentioned that you put what you had learned into practice, into something tangible. It got into my mind that I wanted to go to Europe. At that time, it was unattainable since we did not have money for it. So, I started to visualize the trip. About two days later, a check for a little over $5,000 arrived in the mail. I could not believe it! This was working. That's how I suddenly got caught up in the dark world of the new age. The check turned out to be money for my 401K from my previous job. But I didn't know this in my ignorance.

After the trip to Europe, I returned with a greater desire to practice what I "had learned". I carried the book with me everywhere and shared this knowledge with anyone that would listen. Looking back, it was at this stage the devil subtly deceived me, just like Eve in the garden. I started studying everything mystical, yoga, kundalini, and quantum physics. I enrolled in various self-improvement courses. Even went to a couple of long weekend retreats. My mystical abilities seemed to increase every day. I could guess and predict things that were going to happen in the future. The spirit of divination that had come from my father was now working in me in full effect.

The devil is cunning and makes you believe that these capacities or powers come from you, but it is all a hoax to trap you in his web. The abilities come from familiar demons who know the life of those people and give you the information. Without realizing it, I had become an amateur witch. I interpreted tarot angel cards to my friends, I read their palms, and we would even do hypnosis and talk to doppelgangers. All under the mantle of personal improvement and self-help.

38
"I PROMISE YOU"- DAD

LIFE IN THE UNITED States passed quickly. One day they called to let me know that my dad was admitted to a hospital. Since I was a child, I always saw my father with this awful cough. For me, it was already a part of his personality. I put it down to his bad habit of smoking. I got a little worried since my dad had never been hospitalized for anything. He was a strong man both in character and physically. He always did physical work in construction and carpentry. He was as strong as an oak tree; I never saw him complain about anything. So, I got worried as soon as I heard. I got the hospital's phone number, and I called him. He sounded upbeat and told me not to worry; his exact words were: "I promise when I get out of here, I'm going to quit smoking." I had never heard my dad promise anything. He was a man of his word. That statement put me at ease.

A few days later, someone sent an email from Cuba. The email said that my father had passed away. I felt my heart break into a thousand pieces. How was it possible? Finally, after so many years, they had approved his visa to come to the United States. I fell to the ground crying uncontrollably. Curled up on the kitchen floor like a baby, I cried non-stop. The person I admired the most in this world was gone.

39
"ANGELS FROM BEYOND"

THERE WAS AN INTERNET radio program called: Angels from Beyond. I was fascinated to hear how people called and communicated with "their loved ones" who had already passed away. Every day I'd listen to the program religiously. I tried calling many times, but the lines were always busy. One day my oldest daughter was crying in her room, and I asked her what was wrong. She told me that she missed her grandfather a lot, and I told her to ask to speak with him, that it was possible to do so. I had unknowingly opened another door to the occult. In the Bible, it is absolutely forbidden to want to talk to people who have died and even less to go to mediums or people who communicate with the dead. (Deuteronomy 18:11).

That same afternoon I started listening to the program. As always, I expected to hear a busy signal. I would try calling every day. But that day, I got into the line amazingly fast. I thought: It had to do something with my daughter's request. The devil is very cunning and knows how to hook an entire family. During the call, I told the medium that I wanted to contact my deceased father. The medium was an anglo man in his fifties with a voice that conveyed much peace and security. He immediately began to tell details of my personal life. I really thought I was talking to my dad from the other end. And when he said the following, I was shocked. "Your father says that he is here with your other baby." Tears began to run down my face. How was it possible that my father knew about my abortion? Before he died, I never told him anything about it. This event solidified my belief in the new age, mediums, psychics and other forms of spiritualism. The devil had hooked me.

In their grief for losing a loved one, many people turn to witches or mediums to communicate with their loved ones without knowing they are actually communicating with familiar spirits or demons. The same thing happened with King Saul; in his desperation, he went to meet a witch for information. (1 Samuel 28). This is a very dangerous practice as it opens doors for demons to come to torment your life. In the case of King Saul, that is exactly what happened, and in my case, it was not the exception either.

40
HALLOWEEN

BY THE TIME MY daughters were 14 and 15 years old, Andy and I had been married for almost eleven years and were used to throwing lots of parties at home. We had a two-story, five-bedroom house in San Fernando Valley, California. His TV salary was high enough to pay for the house and give us various commodities. But we always lived from paycheck to paycheck, and the money disappeared as soon as it came in. The house was two stories and one of the largest in the area. Any excuse was perfect to celebrate. We had birthday parties, New Year's Eve, Valentine's Day, Saint Patrick's Day, whatever.

October 31st was coming up, and of course, we had to throw the biggest Halloween party on the block. We invited several of our friends and some acquaintances. We had gone too far with the decoration. From top to bottom, it looked like a haunted house. From the lawn outside to the windows, everything was grossly decorated. Spooky chandeliers, coffins, cobwebs, smoke machines, etc. The worst of the rooms was my youngest daughter's bathroom. We put blood everywhere, fake severed hands and feet, and made the decor a horrific murder scene. The party was "a complete success" with the attendees, and the guests couldn't stop talking about the decor. A few days after that party, my world began to fall apart. I had opened my house to a legion of evil spirits.

41
THE BEGINNING OF THE END

MY YOUNGEST DAUGHTER BEGAN to have behavioral problems. One day I found out she was texting with a guy much older than her. The message had photos and sexual conversations. In another instance, when I picked her up from school, I noticed that she had a sweater on despite how hot it was out. It seemed strange to me, so I asked her about it. She said it was nothing, that she was just cold. I told her to roll up the sleeves of her sweater. To my surprise and horror, she had cut marks in both her arms. She told me she didn't know why she had done it. I immediately looked for a psychologist and began to take her to therapy.

By this point, our marriage was also taking a turn for the worse. Andy and I also went to see a psychologist who was an expert in solving marital problems. The sessions lasted an hour and consisted of questions from the therapist, conflict exercises, and arguments between Andy and I. We both blamed each other, and that's how the sessions went.

I started looking online for love addict groups, and I had to find help for people with the same problem I was facing. I didn't know how to deal with it anymore.

I found a place where several groups of people with different types of addictions met. I entered the building and saw that there were several meeting rooms. I entered the first door. I saw ajar and sat in the back. The tables and chairs in the room were arranged as if it were a school classroom. Suddenly a man stood in front of the monitor and said, "Hello, my name is John, and I am addicted to narcotics." I don't know what else he said afterwards because I was mortified and super embarrassed. How did I get myself into the wrong room? When they took a break, a gentleman approached me to have a conversation, and I immediately realized I was in the wrong place. He asked me: "Which meeting are you looking for?" With all the embarrassment in the world, in a low voice, I told him: Love addiction. The man smiled and told me it was the room next door. I thanked him and went to the exit door, trying to open it carefully so it wouldn't make any noise.

In the next room, there were many more people, about 12 or 15. And they had tables and chairs in the shape of a U. As if it was a presentation room; people took turns telling their stories and chaotic tales. They were very sad stories of divorces and other losses. At the beginning of the meeting, they made a kind of prayer acknowledging that there was a superior being that could help them. In the end, I only went to these meetings a couple of times. Most of the attendees were men, and I didn't feel comfortable sharing my story openly. So, I continued living my life the best I could.

42
THE DJ

ONE OF THOSE NIGHTS, trying to escape from reality, I went to a club on the outskirts of Pasadena, California. There was no trendy nightclub in Los Angeles that I had not frequented, so I drove up there in my thirst for adventure. The place was more of a restaurant that turned into a club at night. I remember going there to celebrate Mother's Day with my daughters.

This particular night I was with a group of friends. Like typical girls, we enjoyed music, taking selfies and catching up on stories about our lives. I remember the music was very good. They played what I liked the most: Reggaeton, electronics, Salsa and so on. At the night's end, someone introduced me to the disc jockey, "DJ

Estelar". He was short and dark-skinned. He wasn't exactly a stud, but he drew attention because he dressed differently, with a leather jacket and well-dressed shoes. With the excuse that we both were into music professionally, we exchanged phone numbers. Soon I found out that he was married. Since I was also married, I felt a certain peace of mind. Despite going out dancing and flirting, the idea of being unfaithful to my husband never occurred to me. It was a purely platonic flirtatious game in my love-addicted mind.

The times I spent with DJ Estelar made me feel alive and vibrant. He was very good at mixing music, and we had a lot of fun. Andy was working a lot and went to El Salvador every so often. Between parties and clubs, a fatal attraction was born between the DJ and I. And from one moment to the next, we felt we could no longer be away from each other. This is the danger of sin, and the devil convinces you that you are not doing anything wrong, and you can get a little closer as long as you do not commit the sin itself. And when you least realize it, you've already been trapped.

43
IF YOU PLAY WITH FIRE...

ANDY BEGAN TO REALIZE my attraction for the DJ. We had endless discussions about it. One night coming back from the club, Estelar was dropping me near the house so Andy wouldn't see who was dropping me off. Estelar parked half a block away from my door when suddenly we saw Andy running straight towards the car, enraged. He started yelling at Estelar to get out of the car. I had never seen him so angry. I jumped out of the car and started trying to diffuse the situation. I grabbed his arm and tried to pull him away from the car. Estelar just put his foot down on the accelerator and sped off.

That wasn't enough for us, we kept texting, and we would spend all our free time together while Andy was working at the TV station.

The DJ's wife had also already figured out what was going on. One day we were at the beach when she called his cell phone. I snatched the cell phone from his hand and answered boldly: Hello! His wife told me: Pass the phone to Estelar. I replied: ``He has nothing to talk to you about; stop calling him". And I proceeded to hang up on her. Estelar got very angry about what I had done, and we started to argue. I told him that he was not going to be playing with me. That he had to choose between his wife or me.

After our argument, Estelar started driving in the direction of my house. The cool summer night breeze caressed my face. Suddenly, a crazy idea crossed my mind, and I said: What do you think if we both get lost? Shall we leave and not look back? His eyes sparkled as if he had asked how he would feel if he had won a Million dollars. For a few minutes, we flew with our imagination. We visualized ourselves together, a life without problems, without worries, and a clean slate. That bubble collapsed as soon as he turned into my block. He parked and told me: "Go back to your husband, Ivet."

44
EVERYTHING COMES TO AN END

MEANWHILE, MY HUSBAND WAS still busy with his work and trips to El Salvador. On the last return trip, he called me from the airport. "Hello love, how are you? I've just arrived." I sensed something was wrong, so I answered abruptly: Do you have something to tell me? Andy replied: We'll talk later when I get home. When he got to the house, he acted like nothing was wrong, but I already knew something wasn't right.

The next day Andy was back to work, but he didn't realize that he had left his phone at home. I didn't think much of it because I had never been the type to be checking a man's phone. But this time, it was different; curiosity kills the cat, so they say. I had a feeling something was going on. When I opened the phone I didn't see anything strange in the text messages. I went to the messengers of different social apps, and nothing; everything seemed normal. I was convinced something was wrong, so I kept looking, and in an application, I found messages between him and a girl from El Salvador. The messages were explicit, and she declared herself to him. I was enraged; my blood was boiling. I called the girl and told her that I wouldn't be fighting for any man and that I gave her permission to keep him. So, I went on Andy's social media and posted a picture of me in a bikini announcing to everyone that I was his wife. As soon as Andy found out, he called me from work. I was brimming with pride at what I had done.

By the time Andy got home, I was already determined to end it all. I told him I would find a real estate agent to sell the house. He claimed that I had pushed him to that. "I responded: You're only mad because I did it to you first." The discussions lasted several days and were endless. He would cry bitterly, but I couldn't help but look at him with a face of disgust and a defiant attitude. My heart was already compromised despite not having been physically unfaithful to him up to that point; and I knew his heart was too. Thus, between arguments and guilt trips, eleven years of marriage came to a halt.

Ultimately, we agreed to sell the house and split the proceeds in half. Several months passed, and the house was not selling. I told my mom about it, and she told me that I had to do witchcraft to accelerate the process of the sale. I started searching the internet on how to do a ritual to attract money. It is incredible how we can find information in the palm of our hands that were previously secrets of the world of the occult. The ritual I decided to do to sell the house consisted of buying sunflowers, honey, or a plate and putting all the concoction in one of the corners of the house. A few days later, we got an offer.

45
AT THE FOOT OF THE ABYSS

SINCE I WAS DIVORCING Andy, I decided to live the high life by renting an apartment in one of the skyscrapers of downtown Los Angeles. With the money from the house sale, I had enough to rent it for a whole year. Estelar went with me, and we filled out the application to rent the place together since he was also separating from his wife. Sometimes he'd stay in another house that he had with his sister. But he would come over to my apartment regularly to hang out or to take me out partying. Deep down, I knew he still wanted to be with his wife, and it was hard for him to separate because of his young daughter. Once I found him in the shower crying, and when I asked him what was wrong, he just cried and sobbed. I knew what was wrong with him. We both had made a huge mistake.

The night of October 31st we began arguing about something; I was already dressed to go out dancing. I was wearing a tight red dress and super high heels of the same color. Clear high heels like the ones pole dancers wear. Even though strip clubs terrified me, I dressed like a stripper, truth be told.

The discussion got so heated that I didn't realize Estelar was already outside the window from one moment to the next. The apartment was on the 15th floor, and we did not have a balcony; it was just a small ledge of only a few inches, which had been made to the building as decoration. No railings or anything; he was just holding on to the window, and his feet barely fit on the edge of the building. When I realized the situation, I turned pale, but something told me not to get close to him. To this day, I believe it was the Spirit of God speaking to me that night. I spoke to him in a shaky, rushed voice from the middle of the room so he wouldn't jump. I would say: "Do you want me to call your sister? Think of your daughter. Don't do it." He was determined and seemed not to listen to me. Suddenly I heard a helicopter in the distance, and I told him: "Please come in! It's the police; you're going to get me in trouble! This seemed to get his attention, and he jumped back into the room.

As soon as his body was inside the room, he jumped on the bed, and I went to hug him. He began to cry and tremble in my arms like a small child, and between sobs, he just repeated: "My angels have abandoned me; my angels have abandoned me." I just thought of comforting him, patting his head while he sobbed in my lap. After a few minutes of reconciliation, we dressed up and went straight to the club.

46
MYSTERIOUS ILLNESS

SOMETIMES I ACCOMPANIED ESTELAR to play at private parties. I would help him unload the console from the car because it was very heavy. They'd hired him to play at clubs, golf courses, mansions, and countless places. On this occasion, we were going to a party for a Latino family in the city of South Gate. As soon as I picked up the console, I felt faint. I quickly told him to put it down on the floor and ran quickly to the bathroom. In that stranger's home bathroom, I looked in the mirror and thought to myself: I'm dying. I felt my body fade away, like when a computer is disconnected from the electric outlet. I told Estelar to take me to the closest Emergency Room immediately. He called my eldest daughter while he was taking me to the hospital, and when he left me with her in the emergency room, he went back to the party since he had to fulfill his commitment.

In the hospital, I had the worst time. The wait was endless, and since they determined I wasn't having a heart attack, they left me lying there for a long time. Since there were so many people and there were no seats available, I had to sit on the cold hospital floor. After waiting a couple of hours, the hospital nurse just said I was dehydrated and gave me a huge cup of water with ice.

After that, I spent about seven months visiting doctors, witches, gurus and other "experts" on the internet, but no one gave a reason for my illness. The first doctor sent me to do a gastrointestinal exam. They sedated me for a couple of hours with anesthesia to insert a camera into my stomach and see if anything was out of the ordinary. They didn't find anything abnormal. The doctor prescribed me some antibiotics and sent me on my merry way.

I paid a specialist in "dark entities" who lived in England, but the appointment took about six months to talk to him. Also contacted a New Orleans witch. I went to an Indian guru who gave me a Reiki massage. One of those massages where they don't touch you, energy massages to "manipulate your energy". It was so bad that I contacted someone from Israel who would heal me by blowing the shofar while repeating some prayers in Hebrew. I also searched for magical healing rituals online and bought many crystals and trinkets. None of it worked, and my health kept deteriorating. By then, I had already spent so much money trying to find a cure, nothing was working, and I was totally broken and desperate.

47
THE WARLOCK

IN A VERY SKETCHY part of the city, there was a botanica. In desperation, I entered the shop full of artifacts to do witchcraft. Although it had been many years since I'd entered a botanica, everything was awfully familiar to me. The smell of tobacco and burnt candles. The many idols and magical amulets. Pictures of many deities, some scary, some innocent and playful looking. There were many people sitting and waiting their turn to talk to the warlock; Sanador was his name, which means Healer, ironically. There was a list where you could write down your name; if they called your name and you weren't there, you would lose your turn until the next day. The first day it took more than an hour, so I left to get something, and when I came back, they had already called me. I returned the next day and put my name on the list. After almost two hours, it was my turn to meet the infamous warlock.

I entered the room where Sanador was, and he was Cuban, just like me, so he had a rapport instantly. It is not a secret to anyone that Cuban sorcerers are known to be "good" at their job. In the middle of the room, there was a small table with a white tablecloth, Healer was sitting at one end, and I sat across from him. The conversation began with Healer giving me an overview of his career as a witch doctor. He told me they had consulted with famous and renowned artists in Hollywood. And even mentioned he had been hired to do a tour to promote a very famous horror movie.

Then it was time to get to why I was there. I told him my dilemma: I was married but had met a guy and left my husband to be with him. The guy was also married, and we didn't know how to get his wife to leave us alone. Healer listened attentively, just like a psychologist is used to listening to his patient's problems. He asked me several questions, and after a while, he started laying out the tarot cards on the table. He began hitting on certain details of my life, earning my trust immediately. All sorcerers work with divination spirits; these are demons that give them information about people. That is why so many people fall into the devil's net without really knowing who they are communicating with.

Immediately after the appointment with Healer. I contacted the DJ, and we decided to meet up that same night. When I got into his car, I was very excited not only to see him but to tell him everything the witch doctor had said about our lives. I began to tell him all the details of what he had told me. And we concluded that we should fight to be together. Since his wife and mother-in-law agreed to make life impossible for him.

As a last instruction, the sorcerer told me to send him photos of me to do the job. Right after I did this, things started to get worse. Let me tell you, and it is a bad idea to send photos of yourself to a witch to do a job. By doing this, you will open a door that you will not be able to close unless it is with the help of God. In my despair and desperation, I went to the witch doctor a second time. This time the recommendation was to do a "limpia". This is a witchcraft cleansing where they give you a bath with water, herbs, or eggs to remove "bad luck". What they don't tell you is that through this ritual, you are opening more doors for demons to come to haunt your life. The limpias for me and Estelar would cost eight hundred dollars. I thought it was a reasonable price to fix all of our troubles.

On the day of my cleansing appointment, they put me in a dark room. A Mexican lady in her thirties saw me this time. She told me that I had to undress completely. I heard that before, Sanador used to do the limpias, but due to a client's complaint of sexual harassment, he stopped doing them. Fortunately, I didn't have to go through the shame of a strange man seeing me naked, but I found myself in such despair that I would have done it anyway, even with him.

Once I was without clothes, she told me to step into a huge round metal bucket with water. I was standing up, and the water was up to my knees. The woman began to pass through my body a bunch of herbs and tobacco smoke. My mind went back to the dozens of times I saw my grandmother in Cuba doing the same thing in her house. She'd hold tobacco with her hand and puff it every once in a while, while on the other hand, she held a bunch of plants and began "cleaning" the walls of her house. Kind of like what people do with sage nowadays. The atmosphere was filled with smoke, and the smell of tobacco permeated everything. I came to hate the smell of tobacco. To this day, I associate it with everything that has to do with witchcraft. But that day, there I was; I was in an environment that was all too familiar. I also remember when I was little, my mother would put me in the bathtub with white flowers. The flower bath session always ended with: "Don't say anything at school." Since my mother was a nurse and belonged to the communist party, this was not something she could participate in. For the communist government in Cuba, members were not allowed to be part of a religion; any religion was forbidden. Only government worship was permissive.

At the end of the cleaning, they gave me a bag with the elements with which they had done the ritual. The bag was plastic and black, along with a small note with instructions. The instructions stated that I had to throw them in front of a Catholic church. I didn't understand why but I was willing to do whatever it took to get rid of the "bad luck".

48
CATHOLIC CHURCH

A FEW DAYS BEFORE the cleansing, I had gone to a Catholic church in downtown Los Angeles. The DJ dropped me off at the entrance, and I headed for the chapel. The mass was celebrated in the English language, led by an American priest. I got there almost to the end of the sermon, so I didn't have to wait long. After the mass, the priest began to greet various parishioners. When the last person left, I shuffled over and said, "I need your help. Can we talk?" In an ironic and mocking tone, he told me: "Do you see me here? Well, I'm not here; I'll take a plane to Europe this afternoon." Disillusioned by the answer, I left that church crestfallen and confused.

So, after the limpia, this was the catholic church I decided I would go throw the suspicious bag at. I didn't dare throw it in front. So, I told Estelar to go to the back of the church, and I threw it into some bushes surrounding the property.

I was totally convinced that my ailments were caused by the witchcraft that the DJ's wife was doing to me. He himself had told me that she confessed to having done a job against us. So, a few days later, I decided to do a ritual against her as payback. I decided to do a ritual for an ex to leave you alone. I shared with Estelar what we were going to do and asked for the items that were necessary. We put everything on a cloth rag, the name of his ex, some nails and a demonic prayer. We tied everything in a knot, and Estelar took him to bury near the train tracks. A few days later, Estelar arrived at the apartment very scared. He said to me: What have you done?! I just came from Margarita's house, and she is very sick; blood is coming out of her eyes. I figured that what Sanador was doing was working, along with our latest ritual. I just answered: "Well, tell her to stop doing witchcraft on us too."

Everything went from bad to worse, so I attended another Catholic church. I was in desperate need of some spiritual answers. I was sure I was going to die from this. This time I went a little more to the entrances of the city. Once again, Estelar left me at the church entrance and left. I walked cautiously inside. As a child, I remember going alone to the plaza in Old Havana and attending the Catholic church to listen to the sermons. In itself, I never understood the message, but I always tried to search for God somehow. I snapped out of that memory and found myself at this new church.

This church was full of candles lit to different "saints". I stopped in front of the Virgin of Guadalupe and knelt before the statue. Scenes from a tv show came to my mind. People on this program would talk about the miracles the virgin of Guadalupe had done for them. Maybe the virgin could do a miracle for me too. I stood there, grieved and heartbroken, and waited for the mass to begin.

The priest had a foreign accent; he was black man with a very charismatic personality. There were fewer people in this church, so I immediately had the opportunity to talk to him after the mass. I told him about my problem, and he kindly welcomed me into his office. He told me that he was from Africa and also spoke some Spanish. He then proceeded to tell me some words that stuck with me: "You are not going to die; I don't know anyone who has come to the Lord in distress and died." Those words gave me encouragement and a desire to continue on. During the second appointment with the priest, Estelar came with me. We told him everything we were going through. We told him that he had left his ex and I had left mine and that we wanted to be together.

We also told him that we suspected that his ex was doing witchcraft on us. Since he was from Africa and familiar with the topics of witchcraft, he was very sympathetic to our situation. Father Benedict just shook his head from side to side and tried to cheer us up. He told me to send him a photo of me with Estelar to continue praying for us. At night I received a text from Father Benedict with our photo next to a homemade altar surrounded by candles. I was somewhat confused since it reminded me of the altars I saw many times in Cuba in the houses of satanic worship. I visited the priest several times and asked him to come to my apartment to bless it.

The first time he came to see me, he brought holy water and a Bible. He sprinkled water all over the apartment and read a couple of prayers from the Bible. Things stayed the same. I asked him to come a second time. Seeing things that did not change, I began to investigate on the internet what other things could cause my ills. Searching the internet, I fell into a black hole of conspiracy theories. It could be aliens, dark entities, and I don't know many other things.

49
MEXICO

I WAS EAGER TO find the reason for my illness, so I went to Mexico to have more medical tests done. Estelar took me to Tijuana, where it is already known that the doctors are more affordable and more knowledgeable. We arrived very early at a clinic in the center of the city. The doctor sent me to another clinic to do X-rays of my brain and chest; they scanned my entire body. By the afternoon, the results were back. I felt nervous but, at the same time, relieved to finally find out what was wrong with me. The doctor looked at me suspiciously and said: "You don't have anything physically wrong with you; I think you have anxiety." We left the clinic without any answers. I knew something was wrong with me, and no one seemed to believe me. Obviously, if the disease was something spiritual, the doctor would not be able to detect it.

Since we were in Mexico, I decided to buy other medicines, including purgatives for parasites. I was desperate and willing to try everything; I would have done anything to be healed. After going to have lunch in a restaurant in the center of the city, we started our way home more confused than when we arrived.

Meanwhile, things with Estelar were going from bad to worse. My health kept deteriorating, and we couldn't figure out how to get any help. He continually looked at me with pity in his eyes. On one occasion, he told me: "They did the same to my mom." I asked him what he meant. "They did witchcraft on her," he said. He was sure his mom died from it. We hugged and cried for a moment.

I became terrified of being alone. I felt like I was going to die at any moment and wanted someone to be by my side in case that happened. Meanwhile, Estelar kept playing for various events and was busy most nights. When he would come back to see me, our connection was not the same. It was more of a caregiver-patient relationship. So, it was the same monotony day in and day out. Go to sleep, hope to wake up and survive another day. The sadness in the apartment was palpable. We didn't know what to do or where to turn to try to get our lives back on track.

50
THE WITCH OF NIGERIA

Estelar introduced me to a woman to get her into a multilevel business we were involved with. I was still very sick, but I was trying my best to work from home. By then, I was living in a brand-new building that had been built in downtown Los Angeles. I had left the other apartment because of the bad memories of Estelar's suicide attempt. This new building was in the city's most modern and hip area. It had all the amenities of luxury living. A Pool, a fully equipped gym, a gourmet market, an organic ice cream parlor, and a vegan restaurant in the lower part. It was the perfect place to have business meetings.

I met the lady in the pool area. She was a very tall woman of a dark complexion, about thirty years of age, with a thin frame and very dark penetrating eyes. At the moment of greeting her with a handshake, I felt a strange current coming from her hand. We talked for about thirty minutes, and then she left. Estelar confirmed what I had felt and told me: "I feel a bad energy with that lady."

A few days later, I invited her to a business conference, and since she had no one to take care of her little girl, I offered for my oldest daughter to watch her in our apartment. When I returned from the meeting, my daughter told me something that made me wonder about her even more. My daughter said that her dog, as soon as he saw the girl, began to bark non-stop. The little girl would have been about four years old. The little girl got scared of the dog and began to say like a mantra: Murder, murder, without stopping. It was another confirmation that something was, in fact, not right.

A few days later, I visited her at her apartment to leave her a product she wanted. Her apartment was close to my house but across the bridge in an area of Los Angeles considered to be unsafe. Upon entering the apartment, I felt like a black blanket had wrapped around me. The air felt dense, and it was almost impossible to breathe with ease. Even though the small apartment was clean and organized, I sensed a foul smell and energy that was hard to describe. I felt very uncomfortable being there.

Because there were already many confirmations of what I felt, I stopped communicating with the Nigerian lady. From then on, she started harassing me. She would call me from anonymous numbers, she would leave me threatening messages on Facebook. Sometimes she would call from an unknown number, and when I answered, she would start speaking in demonic tongues. I immediately recognized that they were demonic languages because that's how my dad spoke when he did his rituals. One of those nights, I dreamed that a witch entered through the window of my room and laughed devilishly. On another occasion, Estelar fell asleep in my bed and told me that he had dreamed that various ghosts were standing outside the window as if they were floating, waiting for something. Since then, paranormal activity in the house began to increase. At night noises were heard in the kitchen, and from time-to-time pots flew and fell to the ground. We were being tormented day and night by spirits. This nightmare seemed never ending.

51
HELP ME, GOD

TIME PASSES SLOWLY WHEN you are sick and at home. Many nights I couldn't sleep as I would wake up drenched in sweat or my hands would go numb. During the day, it was torture to be awake. I couldn't eat anything because my stomach was in a knot, and everything made me want to throw up. I was extremely skinny. I started having episodes of paranoia and agoraphobia. I felt like everyone wanted to hurt me. Because of these paranoid episodes, I almost never left the house.

A Catholic friend of mine recommended that I buy a Bible and open it to Psalm 91. She told me that it was a prayer for protection. My daughter took me to a supermarket, and I bought the first Bible that caught my eye. It was a bible covered in purple leather. I was looking for a bible to read in Spanish, but they only had bibles in English. Although I speak English, I didn't understand anything I was reading.

On June 19, 2015, I was lying in bed browsing social media when something caught my attention. Someone wrote to a murderer telling him that even though everyone hated him, Christ forgave him. The writing was accompanied by a prayer and said that anyone could do it and accept Christ and receive his forgiveness. Without much thought, I began to say the prayer out loud.

"Dear God, I accept that I am a sinner. Please forgive my sins. I believe that you sent your son to earth, he was crucified, but on the third day, he rose again. His death on the cross paid for all my sins. I accept Christ as my Lord and savior. I ask you to write my name in the book of life.

I break every contract with satan and his demons today. Lord Jesus, come into my life, change it, transform it. I pray for all these things in the name of Jesus Christ, Amen."

I can't explain what happened next, but a feeling of repentance and guilt overcame me when I finished saying the prayer. I spent the next forty-five minutes curled up on my bedroom floor, crying and asking God for his forgiveness. Memories came to my mind of how many people I had hurt and how my behaviors had led me to where I was. I felt something inside me had changed when I got up from the floor. The Spirit of God definitely touched me.

52
DELIVERANCE

FROM THAT DAY ON, I couldn't stop reading the Bible. And this time, it was all very clear. I watched dozens of videos of testimonials from people whom God had healed. I kept researching on the internet and found that I might need an exorcism. I immediately contacted the priest who had come to pray for my apartment and told him I needed an exorcism. When we met in person at his church, he told me that this was a complicated process. You had to send a letter to a bishop or something like that, and it would take about two months to get a response. In my desperation, I kept investigating and found that about an hour from my house, a Christian church did something similar to an exorcism, something called deliverance.

DJ Estelar took me to the church since I couldn't drive in my condition. When we arrived there, there were only six or eight people. The pastor was a white man in his fifties and was very calm and well-spoken. After the service, the pastor asked if anyone wanted to come forward for prayer. I walked past and sat in one of the front chairs. An African American lady sat beside me and began praying close to my ear. Suddenly I felt like my left arm bent as if someone was twisting it. That cramp threw me to the floor violently. When I fell to the ground, my body began to twist and turn. My mind was aware, but I couldn't comprehend what was happening to me. The lady stood over me with authority, pointed with her index finger, and said: Let her go! She's not yours! She is not yours! She belongs to Jesus! She started naming and saying things that didn't make sense to me. She said: Witch inside of her, come out now! As soon as she said that, a horrible laugh came out of me. She continued to shout and call out different spirits. A very angry voice came out of me and said: We want to kill her! She continued praying for me. I kept bouncing on the floor like a fish out of water. After a while, I stopped shaking and lay calmly on the floor. The lady helped me and explained that I had been through a process of deliverance.

The experience was so shocking that I decided to learn more about what I had just experienced. I found in the Bible how Jesus had freed people from unclean spirits on several occasions. (Read: Luke 6:18). I began to learn everything that had to do with the gospel and deliverance. For the first time in my life, I understood that age-old war between good and evil. I soon realized that almost no church touched on this very important topic. How was it possible? Jesus spoke and dealt with unclean spirits that tormented people on many occasions. It was documented in all the gospels.

Thus began my search for internal healing. Most deliverance ministers just visited the town for a short time to have special deliverance services. So, I had to go to various places to get delivered. I went with a couple of African American pastors, but they were too loud and intense for my liking. I also went with a minister that was visiting the area and went to his service in Hollywood. The first time Estelar accompanied me. When we entered the room, almost all the chairs were occupied. Anticipation was in the air. We were there with a purpose: to get the demons out of us. Without knowing it, a great spiritual battle was going to be fought. When the minister entered the room, I felt a lot of anticipation. The minister was a chubby white man with a smile that inspired trust and confidence. He recounted his testimony and spoke of the power of The Lord Jesus Christ to cast out demons. And how that power was now in us who had believed in his name and accepted salvation through his sacrifice. (Mark 16:17). Everything was new and interesting, despite having heard it countless times in movies or on the street when someone shared the message of salvation from a corner. This time everything made sense like never before.

After a brief introduction to what we were going to do, the pastor said we would say several prayers out loud. The prayers were meant to break the curses and contracts we made with the Devil. I had unknowingly made many contracts. During one of the prayers, I started to feel uncomfortable, and upon noticing it, the minister came straight to me. Suddenly I was lying on the floor, and he kept expelling unclean spirits. He stopped for a moment and said: What's your name?! And inside me came a voice that said: Margarita! The minister asked: Who is Margarita? He asked a few more times. And Estelar finally said: "She's, my wife." The room seemed to come to a standstill. When we have sexual relations with a person we are not married to, the spirits attached to that person can come to us. The Bible says that we become one flesh with the person with whom we sleep. That is why in the word, The Lord warns man of the danger of joining themselves to a harlot. (1 Corinthians 6:16). It's weird to explain it, but unconsciously I started acting like Estelar's wife. He himself called me on it a couple of times.

After the deliverance, I felt an immediate change. I knew that God was healing me from the inside out. That night the minister made about eight deliverances, including mine. I remember there was a mother and son couple who were also ministered to. The guy was in his early twenties, and he looked pretty unhinged. They mentioned he was schizophrenic. The following week the minister was going to have his last service at the same place. My youngest daughter accompanied me for the second time. On this occasion, we were already more prepared since I had told her about the experience I had had the first time. She also brought in her boyfriend as he was going through some spiritual havoc. Again, I sat in the front row; this time, whatever was left inside of me manifested sooner. The minister noticed something on my face and came over quickly. And he said: unclean spirit inside this woman, I order you to come out now! My face turned into anger and hate.

His next words were: "I order you to get up now!" I don't know how to explain it, but with all my might, I tried to stay seated. Inside me, I thought: Let's see if all this whole show is true. I did everything I could to stay in my seat; but it was not possible, and suddenly I was standing face to face with the man of God. From one moment to the next, something threw me to the ground, and I was spinning around like a rag doll. During the deliverance, my mind was aware, so inside was horrified by what I was experiencing. That night many demons of witchcraft, santeria, palería, jezabel and others came out of me. I have this spiritual battle on video since the guy who accompanied my daughter recorded some of it without me knowing it.

With each release, I felt better. And with each session, I felt like the ties I had in my life were disappearing. In total, I received about ten deliverances from four different ministers. Not surprisingly, since coming from a house where my father was a witch doctor, legions of demons were claiming my life. They did not want to let me go easily, but the Lord took pity on me. Hallelujah!

53
BAPTISM

BY AUGUST, I WAS so in love with The Lord. I felt that the Holy Spirit was telling me that I had to find a church, but in my stubbornness, I would say: "I am fine right here. It's just going to be "You, the Bible, and me". That's how ignorant I was in spiritual matters. The Lord began to press upon me the importance of attending church and equipping myself. It's a fact that satan and his demons have been deceiving humanity for thousands of years. I didn't stand a chance with only a few weeks in the gospel. I would not be able to fight against the forces of evil unless I was planted in a church where the sound doctrine was taught.

Despite not wanting to attend church, I felt the need to be baptized. Since I didn't know any Christian churches around me,

I didn't know where to go. While surfing the internet, an ad for an evangelistic event in Pasadena, CA, appeared "by chance". In that event, they were going to baptize people outdoors, right there in the park. I told Estelar about the event, and he said he would join me and come get baptized too. Through this entire process, Estelar had accepted Jesus. But I knew that it had only been paid lip service. It's like someone who accompanies a friend to see a play that doesn't interest them at all. You only do it to be nice. The day of the event arrived, and Estelar did not show up. My daughters drove me to the christian festival to get baptized.

When we arrived at the park, there were many people in front of a stage; it felt like an outdoor concert. In addition, there were many tents with activities; in some, they prayed for people, and in others, they cut hair, gave food, and took care of children. On the main stage, there were contests, and they were giving out endless prizes, bicycles, toys, televisions, etc. It was a festive atmosphere, and you could feel the love of the workers for the people, but within me, I was heartbroken because I knew that Estelar was not going to show up.

This was an appointment God had set up with me. It was the day that I would publicly follow Jesus forever, leaving worldly things behind. The festival crew had set up several round inflatable pools around the park. Those getting baptized stood in line until it was our turn. The pastors were already ankle-deep in the water. When my turn came, I waited with anticipation for the pastor to dive me into the water. When I came out soaked, people were cheering and applauding, someone handed me a towel, and I began to cry. I knew from that instance that I was a new person. (2 Corinthians 5:17) There was no turning back.

54
I'M NOT GOING BACK

IN THE AFTERNOON, THE DJ called me, explaining why he couldn't attend the baptism; I knew that was the end of our relationship. A few nights before, while I was in my room on my knees praying, I heard God tell me: "I do not change my word for you or anyone else." In my prayer, I asked God to bless my relationship with Estelar, and I told the Lord that he had accepted Jesus and was now a Christian. That was not going to happen because Estelar was still married. The Lord also showed me a Bible verse: Mathew 5:32. This confirmed that we weren't meant to be together.

I felt the Lord telling me: You have three months to break up with him. During those three months, I stopped having sexual relations with Estelar since I became aware that fornication was a sin. Of course, we began to drift apart by removing the one thing that united us.

At the three-month mark, we had a huge argument. In the middle of the yelling match, I told him to man up and end the relationship! He headed for the elevator, and I followed. Arriving in the parking lot in front of his car, he yelled: "It's over!" I turned around and went back to my apartment. I felt a lot of pain and a lot of relief at the same time. That day, I knew I was free and my new life in Christ had begun.

55
ROAD TO HEALING

WITHOUT REALIZING IT, I had a lot of curses surrounding me. During this time, the Holy Spirit began to speak into my life. That is why it is good that we spend time alone with the Lord; that way, he speaks to us, and we listen to him more easily. There alone in my room, the Lord reminded me of the abortion I had had years past. I had to repent of the sin of murder. Whatever the reason for making that decision, I had to regret having agreed to take the life of a human being. It had been around twenty years since my abortion and I had really removed that bad memory from my mind. As soon as I asked the Lord for forgiveness for this transgression, the tears did not stop flowing. It was as if my hard heart was being cleansed from the inside out. Then the calm came, and I felt God's forgiveness and love surrounding me right there in my room.

I asked the Lord what other curses could still be affecting me. He brought to mind that my mom still practiced witchcraft. I immediately called my mother and told her what God had revealed to me. I told her: I will not heal if you still have the door to witchcraft open. I feel the Lord wants you to throw away all the cursed witchcraft objects you have in your house. Only then will I be healthy again. My mom refused. It took me about a month to convince her. One night she took all witchcraft objects she had in the house, put them in a trash bag and threw them into a nearby river. Later, she told me that she heard voices and screams when she tossed the black bag into the river. She then said she got really scared, got in the car, and drove off without looking back. She confessed to me that she was afraid of the consequences of breaking up with the devil, but she agreed to do it for my well-being. The fear of losing her daughter was stronger than the fear of the enemy. It is a fear shared by many Cubans on the Island who are trapped by witchcraft. The Babalawo always scares them with the threat of calamity if they give up on those rituals. This would bring disasters to their economy, to their families and even to their physical bodies. The day she called me to tell me what she had done, I was so proud of her. I reassured her that the devil can't beat Jesus Christ and that now she and the whole family were under the protection of The Lord.

There were many other family curses that I had to break afterwards. Among them were divorce, Freemasonry, Santeria, New

Age, rebellion, etc. It took me about three months to do all the prayers that broke all these chains that surrounded us.

Then came the time to heal the physical. One day while I was watching TV, I internally heard the voice of the Holy Spirit tell me: Get on the internet. By then, I could recognize his voice. I thought to myself: No, I'm watching TV. But this time, the voice said louder: Get on the internet. When I opened the browser on my phone, an article on *mercury poisoning* appeared. Reading it, I couldn't believe it. I had all those symptoms!

Months earlier, I went to a dentist to change my gray fillings to white ceramic ones. The dentist, despite being reputable, had no knowledge of how to extract mercury from the fillings with a safe protocol. So, he didn't use any kind of safety protocol to remove the fillings, and I ended up swallowing and inhaling large amounts of mercury. Unbeknownst to me at the time, I was slowly being poisoned by the mercury that was now in my system. And by the time I started to feel bad, my organs were already full of the deadly poison.

From that moment on, the Lord gradually led me to my physical healing. I went to a naturopathic doctor, but I felt that God told me this was not the right one, and indeed it wasn't. This doctor recommended a treatment to remove the mercury, which was very dangerous. In the end, the Lord revealed my healing to me through an internet group where many people had healed from the same thing. The protocol was invented by a late chemist named Andy Cutler. God's revelation, alongside the Andy Cutler protocol I followed, brought me total healing.

56
THE SAMARITAN WOMAN

ABOUT TWO MONTHS AFTER I started the treatment to expel mercury from my body, I began to feel that I was returning to life. My body was beginning to recover from the ravages caused by this dangerous toxic metal. After spending so much money going to so many doctors, witches, and "spiritual healers", the Lord revealed this protocol to me, and the pill I needed was only about seven dollars at the local pharmacy. I didn't even need a prescription to get it. I soon experienced what the word of God says in Jeremiah 33.3: "Call onto me, and I will answer you, and I will teach you great and hidden things that you do not know." I have absolutely no doubt that The Lord revealed to me the information that healed my physical body.

Now it was time to pursue inner healing. I started spending more time praying, fasting, and reading the word of God. Until I got to John chapter 4. In case you're unfamiliar with the scene, it is by a well. The Lord Jesus asks a Samaritan woman to draw water for him from the well. In those days, the Samaritans and the Jews did not get along. So, it seems strange to her that he would speak to her. In this short conversation, the Lord reveals that she has had five husbands, and none has been her husband. (John 4). There in the living room of my apartment, I began to cry. The Lord Jesus was speaking directly to my heart through these verses. I instantly understood that for a long time, I tried to fill the emptiness in my soul by chasing the attention of any man. I was that Samaritan woman who had gone from relationship to relationship, looking for the love only God could give me. Just like the Samaritan woman in the story, Jesus was telling me that he could give me the only water that quenches thirst forever. At that moment, my soul was being quenched with living water. A soul thirsty for healing, attention, forgiveness, and pure and sincere love.

From that moment, my life changed; I understood why God had saved me. Without knowing it so many years ago, I had made a deal with the Lord on a raft. In an instant, I was reminded of the prayer I had prayed twenty years ago: "If you save us, I will serve you." I felt melancholy. It was the Holy Spirit ministering to my soul. I felt the soft voice of God asking me: What took you so long? That question reached me to the depths of my being. Feeling how the love and forgiveness of the Lord filled every space of my inner being, I felt regret; tears started flowing. I soon found myself on my knees in the living room of my house.

Friend, if you have not yet given your life to Christ, wait no longer. The devil, sooner or later, is going to come to destroy your life and your soul. If you are ready to make the best decision of your life, keep reading the next chapter. It is my greatest wish that you get to experience the peace that only Christ brings. God bless you and guard you. I hope we'll see each other in heaven.

Suppose you are already a Christian; congratulations. If you want to learn more about deliverance and how to liberate other souls, I invite you to continue with the final chapter.

57
DELIVERANCE MANUAL

THIS SHORT SUMMARY IS a preview of the deliverance book I am currently working on. These seven steps are what have helped me in deliverance ministry for the last five years. There is no perfect formula to do deliverance. Let yourself be led by the Holy Spirit and use the authority the Lord has given us to free the captives.

Jesus said that if we have faith as small as a mustard seed, we can move mountains. We don't need any extra tools or tricks to do deliverance—just faith and obedience.

1. Accept Jesus
2. Forgive
3. Renounce contracts

4. Break curses
5. Clean house
6. Maintain your deliverance
7. Be equipped to liberate others

STEP 1.
ACCEPT JESUS

The first step to being free from the invisible chains that bind us and prevent us from accepting Jesus. I remember well that I thought that only people with serious problems needed to accept The Lord. I remember thinking people who were involved in the world of drugs or alcohol were the ones who needed support from the local church. I thought I was a good person; I didn't need salvation from anything. In my ignorance, I did not know that before God, we had all sinned and were far from having a relationship with him. (Romans 3:23) And unknowingly, when we have not accepted the Lord Jesus, we are slaves to sin and satan. (Romans 6:17-19). Accepting Jesus as Lord and Savior is easy and costs nothing. I feel sorry and bad to know that people still spend money on witches and magical amulets, looking for something that only accepting Jesus can bring. Peace, protection, and true love are only found in Christ Jesus.

If you are ready to take the most important step of your life by giving your life to Christ, repeat this prayer out loud:

"Dear Heavenly Father, today I come to you accepting that I am a sinner. Please forgive my sins. I believe that you sent your son

to the earth, he was crucified, but on the third day, he rose again. His death on the cross paid for all my sins. I accept Christ as my Lord and savior. I ask you to write my name in the book of life.

I break every contract with the devil and his demons today. Lord Jesus, come into my life, change it, transform it. These I pray, in the name of Jesus Christ, Amen."

STEP NUMBER 2.
FORGIVENESS

The second and very vital step for complete deliverance is to forgive. Today I have a deliverance group on the Internet, and I always emphasize that the infallible rule for deliverance is that the person must have forgiven everyone who's hurt them. When there is a lack of forgiveness, the person opens doors to the enemy. An unclean spirit of unforgiveness and resentment will open the doors to other worse spirits. (Matthew 12:43-45).

If we are not willing to forgive, The Lord will not forgive us either. (Matthew 6:14-15). I recommend that if there is still unforgiveness, guide the person to renounce the spirit of unforgiveness right away. During this process, the person often begins to manifest, either by coughing, yelling, crying, etc. At this point, we can continue with the deliverance if we see that the person is willing to forgive.

If you need more time to repent of this sin, I recommend that the person being delivered use words of affirmation repeatedly, something like: I forgive (person's name) in the name of Jesus. This process can take days or months, and it is my experience that, little by little, forgiveness will begin to flow from your heart as God heals you through this process.

If the person is not willing to forgive, it is better not to proceed with the deliverance. It is dangerous to do deliverance with unforgiveness still present because the demon of resentment may have rights over the person, and more tormenting spirits will come upon them. (Matthew 12:43-45) It is better to just pray for healing and repentance at this point.

STEP NUMBER 3
RESIGN CONTRACTS

We have all committed several sins. Some we may not even remember. It is true that by coming to Christ, he forgives all our sins. Also true is that sometimes there are sequels and consequences to our sins. For example, if you rob a bank today, and you are heartily sorry, of course, God will forgive you, but chances are that the police will arrest you and put you in jail regardless. The same thing happens in the spiritual world, there are contracts that we have made without knowing, and these carry consequences for us and our relatives. It has been my experience that many Christians, despite having been in the church for many years, still struggle with many problems because they have not obtained deliverance from things they committed in the past. That is why I am sure that the Lord led me through the process of repenting for having had an abortion, committed fornication, made pacts with the devil, and many other sins I had lost count of. When we make pacts with the enemy, he remains there until he is thrown out. Sometimes the person can be set free by the word through praise, reading the word or just repenting, but other times, we have to dig a little deeper. Once I started breaking all contracts and closing all doors to the devil I started experiencing total freedom; and my life started to show fruit.

What contracts am I talking about? There are many ways the enemy can bind us. Let's say that in your innocence, you go one day to have your tarot cards read; there, you have already opened a door for satan to come to torment your life. Another example may be playing occult games or going to a witch or "spiritual healer". A more subtle example can be, lying or stealing to get something; right there you just opened another contract with the enemy, even without realizing it. Every sin committed brings a consequence in the spiritual world, and it is best to close every open door. Many times, during the deliverance session, the Lord reveals to me those contracts that people have made. Therefore, during the session, I lead the person to pray, cancel any contracts, and finally do repentance prayers.

STEP NUMBER 4, BREAKING CURSES

Sometimes, we are unaware that our ancestors could have opened a door. For example, my family made many animal sacrifices to Satan. I know of cases where the ancestors' made sacrifices or murdered people. These are very big curses that need to be broken in the name of Jesus. When the person confesses and cuts these contracts, Satan cannot retain the life and future of this person and that of their family. There are also curses for having committed fornication or having had a child out of wedlock. I have seen that many times, these sins bring curses of poverty and calamity.

STEP NUMBER 5
CLEAN HOUSE

A very vital step after converting is to clean your home. And I don't mean with soap, bleach, and water, but spiritually. Of course, before we come to Christ, we had no idea that some things are anathema. The Bible calls anathema any object that is cursed. When we live in the world, we bring a lot of objects into the house that are unknowingly casting a curse on our lives. Sometimes, our friends and family unknowingly give us things that are cursed too.

In my case, it took me about nine months to remove everything that I had accumulated for years. The Holy Spirit revealed to me everything I had to take out of my house that was anathema, including clothes, shoes, books, music and movies. Some of the things I remember throwing away were skull suspenders, sky-high black heels that also had corpses paved in the heel, headless mannequins I had at my previously owned clothing store, and a $300 bottle of perfume that came in a case with a golden snake. Without realizing it, I had surrounded myself with things that filled my house with curses, but when we do not have the revelation of the Holy Spirit, we walk blindly and are slaves of satan.

There are very common objects that attract curses to homes; I have often found them in Christian homes as well. Some of these objects are Buddha statuettes, dreamcatchers, stones to attract love or money, prosperity, new age books, santeria or witchcraft books, saints, idols, horror movies, music with vulgar or aggressive vocabulary, clothes with hate images, paintings or pictures of worldly celebrities. There is an infinity of objects that can be anathemas. Ask the Holy Spirit to reveal everything that should come out of your house. After throwing all these items in the trash, (please do not even think of giving or donating any of this to other people), use anointing oil and say a prayer for your home, sanctifying and setting apart your family for the Lord. This works very well when a family is going through some type of torment, such as "bad luck", noises in the night, night attacks, nightmares, or some other spiritual attack. But remember that the first step is to accept Jesus as your Lord and Savior. If you don't take this first step, you don't have any kind of spiritual authority to cast the demons out of your home, and they know it.

STEP NUMBER 6
HOW TO STAY FREE

Once you and your family have been freed from the clutches of the enemy, it is vitally important to learn how to maintain your deliverance. There are things that I am going to mention that are not negotiable. Once you feel better and trust yourself, an attack may become even worse than the previous one. So, pay attention; these are the ways that you will keep your freedom. First of all, you must turn away from sin. Once you receive salvation and deliverance, you must leave your old life behind. If you fornicate, don't fornicate anymore; if you take drugs, don't do drugs anymore, as the case may be. Seek help from a group of Christians who have been through the same thing and are now free. If you continue to sin consciously after being delivered, your condition may worsen. (Mathew 12:43-45)

Start reading God's word every day. For me, my preferred and reliable Bible is the King James version. When you are a baby in Christ, you must learn how to defend yourself against the enemy's attacks. The word of God is that spiritual sword you will need for this spiritual battle. (Hebrews 4:12) Find a Christian church that teaches sound doctrine and properly explains the basic concepts of Christianity, salvation, repentance, forgiveness, grace, communion, sacrament, the concept of the Trinity, and other Christian teachings. I also recommend that you start hearing worship songs all the time. In the car, when you go to work, at home, even when you leave the house from time to time, leave a radio playing praises, the demons cannot stand it; and consequently, they will leave any place filled with praise and adoration towards God.

Lastly, you must begin to meet and fellowship with other Christians who are more mature in the faith. This is vitally important, as this support group will help you with prayer, encouragement, and friendship through the ups and downs of life. A lonesome Christian is like a solitary sheep that inadvertently strays from the flock; the wolf perceives it in the distance and stealthily begins to chase it. Eventually, the wolf ends up catching up with her and devours the strayed sheep. Please don't be that lost sheep; the end result can be disastrous. The enemy has been around for thousands of years, which is why he has more experience than you and me. Let's not be naive, believing that we can only fight off the forces of evil being fed every once in a while with an online sermon. There is strength in unity, and the enemy knows this very well. (Ecclesiastes 4:7-12)

STEP NUMBER 7
FREE THE CAPTIVES

Once we are mature enough, it is time to free others. In the corporate world, I learned that the best way to retain what you have learned is to teach others what you have learnt. "Teach to Teach ", they call it. In my case, almost a year after I converted, I had already given my testimony on a Christian radio station. After two years, I already had a group of people to whom I gave deliverance classes weekly. A word of warning: Don't wait too long for the perfect moment to evangelize or lead a group. Once the Lord gives you the signal, it is time to go out and share the message of salvation. If you don't, you run the risk of getting stuck without any purpose. It is very sad to see how many Christians have been deceived by satan and only go to church on Sundays to listen to the word or greet people as if it were a social club. The enemy lies to many by telling them that they are not ready, that they do not have time, that they are too busy, or that they are not sufficiently prepared to do a ministry. Don't over-complicate it; learn, and teach at the same time. There are many people out there who need deliverance, even within the church. Let the Lord use you.

DELIVERANCE PRAYERS

Below, you will find deliverance prayers that helped me get delivered from the generational curse and other occult practices. Remember that before doing these prayers, you must first accept Jesus as Lord and savior by doing the salvation prayer. It is very dangerous to say these prayers if you are not part of God's family.

Salvation Prayer

"Dear Heavenly Father, I admit that I am a sinner. Today I ask your forgiveness for my sins. I admit and acknowledge Jesus as my Lord and Savior. You sent him to earth, and he was crucified, but on the third day, he rose again. Lord Jesus, come into my life, change it, transform it. From now on, I have decided to follow you every day of my life. Amen."

Prayer to get out of the occult

Father, forgive me for opening my door to satan through any occult practice. At this time, I confess and repent from having practiced witchcraft, santeria, played Ouija, burned incense to false gods, and put my trust in stones, horoscopes, and or astrology. I repent from having practiced yoga, read tarot cards, and consulted witches, mediums, or fortune tellers. In the name of Jesus, I break every contract made with satan and his demons through these practices. I thank you, Father, for freeing me from every curse of occultism in the name of Jesus Christ. Amen.

Prayer to be able to forgive

Father, in the name of Jesus, I decided to forgive every person who has hurt me. Just as you have forgiven me, I forgive that person(s). I lose myself from any relationship with the evil spirit of unforgiveness. From now on, I decide to forgive with all my heart in the name of Jesus Christ. Thank you, Lord, for freeing me from any curse that has come into my life due to unforgiveness. Help me to have a clean heart, free of evil, hatred, and grudges, in the name of Jesus. Amen.

Prayer to cancel Generational Curses

Father, I ask that, in the name of Jesus, you release my relatives and me from all generational curses. I ask for your forgiveness for our contract with the enemy throughout the generations. We cancel any contract, blood covenant, or sacrilege committed by any ancestor in the name of Jesus. The blood of the lamb has paid for our sins, and the enemy no longer has the power to act against us. We close every open door and seal it with the blood of Jesus. Lord, today we make a pact with you; my family and I have decided from now on to follow only you. We venerate your holy name. We will dedicate our lives to your service. Help us to love you above all things. In the name of Jesus. Amen.

ABOUT THE AUTHOR

Ivet Fortun was born in Havana, Cuba. At the age of 14, she left the island on a raft with her mother and brother for the United States.

She has a degree in social sciences with a specialty in psychology from California State University Los Angeles. She is married to a great man of God, Isaías Rodríguez, and has two grown daughters and three precious grandchildren. She currently works as a real estate investor and is dedicated to the ministry of deliverance and health, where she is training others how to set captives free through the power of God.

Made in the USA
Las Vegas, NV
13 January 2024

84229922R00095